"We guys want to read a [...] Great
Being a Dad is a simple ([...] want
to be. Hey, friend, read i [...]

.emp

vice president of FamilyLife, former NFL quarterback,
and author of *Facing the Blitz*

"*It's Great Being a Dad* is fun, easy to read, and full of practical wisdom and truth. Carey, Brock, and Jay share stories and humor that encouraged me, challenged me, and reminded me of the great joy and privilege it is to be a dad. I am inspired and energized to finish strong!"

Francis X. (Frank) Kelly III
CEO of Kelly Financial Services

"This book is one more example of the important work being done by my friend Carey Casey and the hardworking team at the National Center for Fathering. I recommend *It's Great Being a Dad* to any father who loves his kids."

Dayton Moore
general manager, Kansas City Royals

"Whether your father was a stellar example or a missing part of your life, this book is an excellent tool for becoming the father God has called you to be and the positive influence your community needs."

Rodney Bullard
executive director of Chick-fil-A Foundation

"Being a parent is a true blessing from God. *It's Great Being a Dad* is a book with simple and yet terrific practical applications for dads."

Darrel Billups
executive director of National Coalition of Ministries to Men

"This book is an amazing testimony of God's call to fathers as our children's primary life and spiritual leaders. It pulls at the heartstrings and confirms what millions of men already know and what many more are waiting to experience—*it's GREAT being a dad!*"

Matt Haviland
founder and director of A Father's Walk, a ministry to single dads

"Fatherhood brings irreplaceable duties and incredible delights, and *It's Great Being a Dad* highlights both through realistic short stories and practical insights. No matter what stage of fatherhood you are in, this book will encourage and equip you to be the dad your child desperately needs you to be."

Wayne Simien
NBA world champion, campus minister with Called to Greatness

"Imagine having Carey, Brock, and Jay as your personal coaches while hearing their insights about being a proactive dad from their collective years of experience in the trenches as invested fathers. *It's Great Being a Dad* gives practical, proven, interactive ideas that you can put into action today."

Michelle Watson, PhD, LPC
author of *Dad, Here's What I Really Need from You:*
A Guide for Connecting with Your Daughter's Heart

"This is the perfect dad-book. The chapters are short, the stories powerful, and the advice is *real*. No doubt about it, being a dad is hard…this book reminds us that it's also great being a dad. I give it the Familyman's Seal of Approval!"

Todd Wilson
Familyman Ministries

"You're welcome—because after you read *It's Great Being a Dad*, you are going to say thank you! Being a dad is hard. Let my friends Jay, Brock, and Carey help you learn the art of fathering. You are going to love this book as much as I do."

Derwin L. Gray
lead pastor, Transformation Church
author of *Crazy Grace for Crazy Times* Bible study

"You'll get plenty of food for thought in *It's Great Being a Dad*. In fact, you'll get an entire buffet. Trouble is, once you start digging in, it's hard to stop."

Tim Shoemaker
author of *Super Husband, Super Dad:*
You Can Be the Hero Your Family Needs

"A father's role in the life of his kids, for good or bad, is inestimable, and it's never too late to start making a difference. Jay, Carey, and Brock have brought together inspiring and empowering concepts for every dad to put in place to make today count for our kids. Thanks for this great resource!"

Tony Rorie
founder of Men & Ladies of Honor

"As one of my mentors would have said, 'This book is delicious!' Each chapter can be consumed in a few small bites, reminding us of how important our role of father is and motivating us to be the best dads we can be."

Tom Pearce
national director of Shepherding the Next Generation

"Jay, Carey, and Brock have hit a nerve that touches every dad who wants to be a great dad—how to be intentional. This book is packed with powerful, doable examples of what it means to be intentional. This ought to be in every dad's toolbox!"

Cavin T. Harper
founder and executive director of Christian Grandparenting Network

IT'S GREAT BEING A DAD

JAY PAYLEITNER, BROCK GRIFFIN, AND CAREY CASEY,
CEO, THE NATIONAL CENTER FOR FATHERING

HARVEST HOUSE PUBLISHERS
EUGENE, OREGON

Cover by Writely Designed

Cover photos © Fotofermer, Aleksandar Mijatovic / Fotolia

Jay Payleitner is published in association with the Steve Laube Agency, LLC, 5025 N. Central Ave., #635, Phoenix, Arizona, 85012.

This book contains stories in which people's names and some details of their situations have been changed to protect their privacy.

IT'S GREAT BEING A DAD
Copyright © 2015 the National Center for Fathering
Published by Harvest House Publishers
Eugene, Oregon 97402
www.harvesthousepublishers.com

Library of Congress Cataloging-in-Publication Data
    Payleitner, Jay K.
    It's great being a dad / Jay Payleitner, Brock Griffin, and Carey Casey, CEO, the National Center for Fathering.
      pages cm
    ISBN 978-0-7369-6296-4 (pbk.)
    ISBN 978-0-7369-6297-1 (eBook)
    1. Fatherhood—Religious aspects—Christianity. I. Title.
    BV4529.17.P396 2015
    248.8'421—dc23
                           2015024241

Printed in the United States of America

15 16 17 18 19 20 21 22 23 / BP-CD / 10 9 8 7 6 5 4 3 2 1

In tribute to (and in memory of) our own dads,
—Ken Payleitner, Leland Griffin, and Ralph Casey—
who showed us how to be good dads
and continue to teach and shape us even today.

ACKNOWLEDGMENTS

It's great being a dad. And it's great to work in an environment that lifts up the role of fatherhood. We are very aware that the "work" at the National Center for Fathering (NCF) is much bigger than we are.

As we endeavor to inspire and equip dads, so often we find ourselves inspired and equipped by others, such as the children who write priceless essays about their dads and all the dads who truly live out what this book is about with their children. We are thankful beyond measure for—and greatly humbled by—the faithful involvement of the NCF board of directors and many others who partner with us as trainers, volunteers, and/or financial supporters.

Through the years, so many wonderfully gifted individuals have been part of our team here at NCF. Currently on our hardworking staff are Steve Wilson, Brian Blomberg, Sherri Solis, Bea Peters, Chelsea Mudd, Steve Stiffler, and Yemescrach (Yemi) Wendemagegnehu. Our dedicated crew at WATCH D.O.G.S. (Dads of Great Students) includes Eric Snow, Shelly Perry, Chris Danenhauer, Frank Hannon, Denise Griffith, Gloria Vaquera, and Keith Schumacher.

The authors are also grateful to agent Dan Balow for his patience and persistence. And to the faithful and accomplished team at Harvest House Publishers, including Gene Skinner, Terry Glaspey, and Bob Hawkins Jr.

From Carey: I am thrilled to acknowledge a few people who have influenced me to contribute to the writing of this book. I will forever be grateful for Mom and Pop, who modeled parenting and a strong marriage for me. I thank God for my bride, Melanie, who has given me four wonderful children. I have fun being a dad of three adult children and a teenage son, Chance, who came 14 years later and is now off at college. As I often state, Chance keeps my fathering fresh. Thanks to Ken Canfield, our founder at NCF, for casting the vision and setting the course. And to all of the influencers who loved me, coached me, and modeled for me the importance of my role as a dad, thank you for your encouragement and support.

Brock sends his love and thanks to Tara, Cole, Brooklyn, and Devan—for making the journey so satisfying and for their patience and grace for a husband and father who is still growing. And to Dad and Mom (Leland and Janet Griffin) as well as Virgil and RuthAnn Warren and the entire Warren clan—for their continuing support and encouragement. To pastors and friends at Legacy Christian Church—for living the Word and helping us do the same. Also to Ken Canfield and Carey Casey, leaders at NCF—for creating space for me to use my gifts, for continuing to affirm those gifts, and for being key friends and mentors for fathering and for life.

Jay sends his gratitude to his growing family—Rita, Alec, Lindsay, Randall, Rachel, Max, Megan, Isaac, Kaitlin, Rae Anne, Judah, Jackson, and Emerson. You inspire and motivate me. I love you all.

And to our Savior, Jesus, who went to the cross for each and every one of us. Without your perfect love and perfect plan, none of this makes any sense.

Contents

Introduction

We think being a dad is just about the greatest, most rewarding job in the world. And we want you to feel the same way.

On the book cover are the names of Jay, Brock, and Carey. But this book is actually a labor of love inspired by the millions of dads who have been touched by the work of the National Center for Fathering (NCF).

We love each one of those guys. We love every desperate dad who has walked through our doors looking for help. We love the men who have gone through our workshops and small-group training sessions and have committed to Championship Fathering. We applaud and appreciate the men whose names are inscribed in our Fathering Hall of Fame and who volunteer in their kids' schools through our WATCH D.O.G.S. initiative. We care deeply for thousands of dads who read our weekly blogs and sit in audiences inspired and challenged by NCF speakers. We are humbled that millions of men have tuned in to *Today's Father* broadcasts five days a week on hundreds of stations since 1993.

We pledge to expand our impact through books, e-books, essay contests, fathering court, and winsome social media campaigns. And we take seriously our responsibility to conduct groundbreaking research that helps shape national policy and impacts fathers and families across the country.

Are you with us? We'd like to stand shoulder to shoulder with you.

Representing the National Center for Fathering, we coauthors have logged untold hours researching, writing about, speaking on, advocating for, and simply pondering the concept of fatherhood. Carey Casey has headed NCF since 2006. Brock Griffin is the writing and publications director, having served on staff since 1991. Bestselling author, speaker, and producer Jay Payleitner has been affiliated with NCF for more than two decades. Altogether we have 12 children. Carey and Jay may or may not be adding grandchildren even as this book goes to press.

As you read, the collective voice you hear is ours. Carey, Brock, Jay. Despite all our experience—as fathers and as men who work with dads—we are far from perfect. We make our share of mistakes. We don't have all the answers. But that's the point and purpose of the National Center for Fathering and all we do. As dads, we're all in this together. We need to share ideas, take risks, lift each other up, ask forgiveness, and admit we need help sometimes. Ultimately, we need to depend on the power and presence of our heavenly Father. Otherwise, even our best efforts are going to fall way short.

So keep reading. We promise the wonderfully imperfect insight that follows is going to make you a better dad. It's all based on personal experience, interviews with thousands of dads, a vast amount of primary research, national polls commissioned in partnership with other organizations (including Gallup), and biblical authority.

You'll be glad to see we're using a format of short chapters that cover a lot of ground. That allows us to draw on the power of story and deliver user-friendly truths on a variety of topics without getting bogged down in one area. If you find one chapter doesn't apply to your situation, keep reading. Within a few pages, we'll be venturing down a new path. That's the approach we've been taking with our daily radio broadcast, weekly blogs, and social media posts, and it's clearly working.

Finally, we hope that somewhere along the way you have been (or will be) presented with a lovingly chosen or handmade coffee mug, pencil holder, or T-shirt that says, "#1 Dad" or "Father of the Year" or

"It's Great Being a Dad." Sentiments like that may sound cliché, but you can be sure that the young gift giver totally depends on you for guidance, adventure, unconditional love, and a roof over their head.

We desperately want all dads to experience greatness at every age and stage of fatherhood. We know firsthand that fathering can and should be a blast.

"It's great being a dad."

—CAREY CASEY, BROCK GRIFFIN, AND JAY PAYLEITNER

1

Kid Fix

Bob can't help himself. He has all the signs of severe addiction. Bob is a pastor and a father. This is his story.

His church staff first noticed it one day during a meeting. The discussion was intense, but Bob's eyes started wandering. "Bob," someone said, "did you hear me?"

"Oh…sure," he said, and his focus snapped back to the person's face. He leaned forward to study some papers on the table, and the meeting resumed.

A few seconds later, the withdrawal symptoms were more than Bob could take. Someone was in the middle of a sentence, and Bob stopped him. "I'm really sorry," he said, "but I just can't concentrate. Hold your thought, because we need to get through this. I just need to step out for a minute." And out the door he went.

The other people in the meeting were left with a confused look on their faces. Where could he have gone, and why couldn't it wait 20 minutes?

They waited. Angie twiddled her thumbs, Brianna crossed and recrossed her legs, Jason offered to get coffee.

Seven or eight minutes later, Bob shuffled back into the room. "Where were we?" he said. Everyone just looked at him, still perplexed.

"Okay," he said, "I'm sorry I left, but I couldn't wait. My kids are down in the day care, and I just had to have a kid fix."

Dad, has that ever happened to you? We hope so. It's one of the great rewards of being a dad.

But be warned. *Fatherhood is addicting.* Maybe you'll start with bouts of all-star wrestling when you get home from work. Before you know it, you'll be sneaking hugs before dinner, lingering at their bedside after prayers, and uttering words of encouragement when they leave for school. If you miss that opportunity to score a fix, you may have to resort to Bob's method—you'll call home in the middle of the day just to talk to your children. And then, if worse comes to worst, you'll become a pusher, like us.

At NCF, we plead guilty to being obsessed with promoting and peddling the powerful father-child addiction. And we also apologize for taking that analogy this far. We know far too well harmful addictions are tearing families apart. But don't miss the point.

Your children are precious and adorable creatures. We could go on and on about how they benefit from your involvement, consistency, and affection. They need you, and that should be enough motivation to be a good dad.

But we'll tell you—and Pastor Bob will concur—there are some incredible rewards for you as well. Plain and simple, fathering is a high like no other.

Go home tonight and get a healthy dose of your children. It may be a mind-expanding, psychedelic experience that changes your life. And theirs.

> *"Children are a gift from the Lord;*
> *they are a reward from him."*
>
> **—PSALM 127:3 NLT**

2

Rainy Days

During a recent rainstorm, a young woman named Alice listened to a friend complain about the dreary weather. "It's like the world stops and you're trapped."

After a reflective pause, Alice gave an easygoing reply. "I love the rain."

"What? You like this weather? I can't imagine why."

Alice explained, "When I was a little girl, my dad was a carpenter, and he did a lot of jobs outside. So if it was raining, I knew there was a good chance Daddy couldn't leave for work that day. He'd be home, in his little shed out back, and I could be with him as he did his woodwork."

She continued, "So now, a nice rainy afternoon brings all that back to me, and I have those same feelings of spending time with my dad and being close to him. When it rained, that meant he would be there for me."

Can you picture that little girl? Cherishing that time with her daddy. Can you see her now as a young adult? Smiling at the memories. Most fathers don't fully understand how much our children long for our time and attention or how much they simply want to be *with* us. Really, the best time we spend with them is not go, go, go. Memories are made doing simple, everyday activities together—weeding the garden, painting the porch, playing catch, or driving to the hardware store. You know, just hanging out.

For Alice, those times with her dad will be with her the rest of her life. Every time it rains, she feels special. The question to consider is how you can have that kind of impact on your children.

One clue from Alice's story is that she connected a regular event with a sense of expectation. Rain will forever be linked with time spent together with her dad. And memories were made. What's really interesting is that Alice's dad probably didn't even know he was creating images and emotions that would last a lifetime.

It's possible, Dad, that you're well on your way to making similar memory links with your kids. On Sunday mornings, do you read the comics together? On clear nights, do you point out constellations? During snowstorms, do you huddle together around the fireplace? When you're checking the fence line, do you make sure you have a son or daughter riding shotgun? When the Red Sox game is on, do you make room on the couch?

If that describes time spent with your child, then decades from now that grown-up kid will have plenty of moments that trigger memories of time with Dad and bring a warm smile and a wash of nostalgia. A Sunday newspaper, starry night, snowstorm, visit to a hardware store, or ball game is all it will take.

We encourage dads to be intentional about initiating activities and spending time together with their kids. When the kids are young, it's easy. They are eager to tag along, snuggle, or be Daddy's helper. As they get older, you'll want to find a regular time and place where your world intersects with their world—a hobby, a sport, a small business, an intellectual pursuit, or work where you get some good honest dirt under your fingernails.

Don't wait for a rainy day, Dad. With a little effort, you can begin to make some easygoing memories with your children this very week.

> *"Time spent with Dad doesn't have to be jam-packed with activities. Maybe the activity is just spending time with Dad."*
>
> **—BROCK GRIFFIN**

3

Airport Skipping

Ever see a normal-looking guy doing something really goofy? Chances are it had something to do with a kid.

Patrick was leading his family through an airport terminal as they were moving to a different city. He held on to his six-year-old daughter's hand as they made their way to a connecting flight.

Suddenly his daughter got an excited look on her face and looked up at him. "Daddy," she said, "let's skip!"

Now, you can imagine what went through his mind: *Hmm. In dozens of flights, I've never seen a 38-year-old businessman skipping through an airport. Maybe it has happened and I just missed it, but probably not.*

This was no earth-shattering moral dilemma, and yet the idea of skipping through an airport with his daughter really made him uncomfortable. Why? Are grown-ups banned from skipping? Would he see someone he knew? Or maybe the airport etiquette police would take him away on a cart with flashing lights.

But then Patrick realized maybe there was something higher at work here—higher than reputations and appearances and looking silly in public. Maybe he could pull off this one frivolous stunt and make a little girl happy. Maybe he could help her forget for a few minutes that she wasn't all that excited about moving anyway.

That's what committed dads do. We put our children's desires above our own. And sometimes it isn't easy. We may risk looking silly to put a bright spot in our daughter's day. We risk forgoing advancement at work so we can spend more time with our children. Maybe we put a hold on our weekend plans because little Jackson wants to go visit a space museum on Saturday afternoon.

That isn't to say we let our children run our lives or that we hesitate to correct them when they need it. But maybe we should adjust our thinking so that our first thought is to give our children the desires of their hearts whenever those desires aren't for something harmful. We believe that's how God, our heavenly Father, responds to us.

And by the way, if you ever hear about some crazy, middle-aged guy skipping down the airport terminal, just remember, it made a six-year-old girl mighty happy.

> *"Truly I tell you, unless you change and become like little children, you will never enter the kingdom of heaven."*
>
> **—MATTHEW 18:3**

4

Make Your Home a Hangout

Who does your teenager hang out with? And where do they hang?

It's inevitable. As children become teenagers, their friends play a more influential role in their lives, and fathers typically spend less time with their kids. But that doesn't mean fathers are less important.

One of the best ways to stay in touch with your teenagers is to acknowledge their friends are important and get to know them. It's all part of being an aware father. Can you name your daughter's three or four closest friends? What sort of mood is your son in after spending a day with his best friend? What positive and negative influences are they picking up?

If you really want to know your kids better, get to know their friends. And look for the positive qualities your child sees in them. You probably can't come right out and ask your child to list the character qualities of their friends. But if those friends are in reasonably close proximity on a regular basis, eventually you will begin to know what makes them tick.

Here's the plan. By definition, kids want to spend time with their friends. They can be together at the mall, at the friend's house, or somewhere else. Or they can be at *your* house. Simply stated, if you want to maximize your influence on your children and their friends, make your home a hangout. It might take a little work and a small financial investment.

Stock your kitchen with healthy snacks kids like. And maybe also a few quarts of ice cream and their favorite chips. Have some fun things to do that don't necessarily involve electronics. Maybe a basketball hoop, a Ping-Pong table, board games, art supplies, a fire pit, a hot tub…whatever does the trick. If you think video games are essential to creating a welcoming environment, then be proactive. Do a little research and find games that are fun, popular, and family friendly.

With older kids, give them some room to breathe. Make your presence known from time to time, but don't expect to provide constant supervision. Instead, establish a pattern of checking in, walking through, dropping off a hot pizza, coming back with napkins ten minutes later, picking up a magazine, checking on the dog, asking about your teenager's schedule the next day, and so on. Don't be a pest, but establish the fact that your home is a home. And your family is a family. And Mom and Dad are part of the package. Believe it or not, young people crave family and the involvement of caring parents. Many of your children's friends may not experience that at their own address.

Worth mentioning, there's a trend in some communities of "cool parents" providing alcohol to underage children right in their home. The excuse is that kids are going to drink anyway, so they might as well be safe about it. We urge you not to give in to such foolishness. It's illegal, and it sends a message that leads to even worse decisions down the road.

As an aware father, you're on a quest to observe (but not to control) the many facets of your child's life. The more information you have, the better chance you have to protect them and guide them to better life choices. You'll quickly pick up on potentially harmful habits or influences, and you'll also discover new ways to relate to them and form a closer connection. That mutual respect will create a bond that will very likely last a lifetime.

"No matter where they go, what they do, or who they become, make sure your children always carry with them a little piece of home."

—JAY PAYLEITNER

5

Extreme Fathering

They jump off bridges held by nothing more than a glorified rubber band. They ride fat-tire bicycles at breakneck speed over steep and treacherous terrain—sometimes in snow. They jump out of airplanes with a small board attached to their feet and surf the wind, waiting until the last possible second to deploy their parachutes.

These thrill seekers are participating in what have come to be called extreme sports. The activities are "extreme" because they're radical, spine tingling, and on the edge. You see them in soda commercials trying to make you think that these guys are living life to the fullest and having a great time.

Of course, all these dangerous activities will make your heart race, and you'll fear for your life. But from our perspective, it isn't truly engaged living. Those daredevil acts are nothing compared to the most extreme activity that a man can engage in—that's fathering.

G.K. Chesterton wrote about the "wildness of domesticity," and French poet Charles Péguy described it this way:

> Family life is the most "engaged" life in the world. There is only one adventurer in the world...the father of a family. Even the most desperate of adventurers are nothing compared with him. Everything in the modern world...is organized against that fool, that imprudent, daring fool...against the unruly, audacious man who is daring enough to have a wife and family.

Why is fathering extreme? Because so many sectors of our culture *don't* reward you for placing a high priority on your home life. Because it isn't "cool" for men to spend time at the water cooler talking about how they can improve their communication skills with their children. Because there are huge risks and huge rewards.

Committed fathers are the ones who are really "out there" and "on the edge"—and you don't even have to wear expensive goggles and get helmet hair. You don't have to free-fall from a plane or hurl your body down a mountainside. You don't even have to leave home.

You just have to do what's already in your heart—devote yourself to your children with wild abandon.

That's one of life's greatest thrills and adventures. That's what really takes courage. That's truly engaged living. And that's extreme.

Go for it, dude...er, that is, Dad.

> *"My heart breaks for men who walk away from opportunities to engage in fathering because they're looking for something that's more fulfilling."*
>
> **—CAREY CASEY**

6

Scrubbing the Cat

You wake up at three twenty in the morning and hear your six-year-old daughter calling out. "Mommy! Daddy! My tummy hurts!" You know what that means, and you don't even think about elbowing your wife. You get up and go check on your little girl.

It turns out she has thrown up in the bed…and on the family cat. The cat is nowhere to be found, but it left a dreadfully obvious trail for you to follow. So there's a little girl to wash up and comfort, sheets and blankets to wash, carpet spots to clean, and a very angry and frightened kitty to capture.

And you do it all. All by yourself. Why? Because you're a dad, and this is one way you express your love. Oh, we know. Love is the last thing you feel at four a.m., but that doesn't matter. Loving feelings are not required to do loving acts. It's also a loving act toward your wife to let her sleep.

In Matthew 6, Jesus tells us, "Where your treasure is, there your heart will be also." In context, it's pretty clear that he's talking about heaven, where moth and rust cannot destroy our inheritance. But the principle also applies to things we value here on earth.

Put another way, when you place high value on your family, your heart will follow. Practically speaking, even if your heart isn't completely into it, go ahead and act like a committed dad and husband. Suddenly your heart becomes filled with purpose and joy.

Put even more succinctly, loving feelings will follow loving actions.

A marriage counselor might tell a struggling couple to do caring and even romantic things for each other even if their feelings aren't in it. The feelings will follow.

As fathers, we're often asked to do things that aren't fun, convenient, comfortable, or on our list of preferred activities for the evening or weekend. Initially, they don't feel like love.

We help with homework. We care for a sick child. We have that hard talk with our teenager. We assemble a bunk bed from IKEA. We give our Lakers tickets to a friend because our son has his own biddy basketball game that night. We drive and drive and drive some more. We change a diaper.

We do what needs to be done. And there are no regrets.

I hope you see how that works. The secret to loving your child isn't waiting until the feeling arrives and then acting. It's knowing what's right, knowing what your child needs, and doing it. Love is more about commitment and determination than feelings.

Oh, yeah—and by all means, be careful washing the cat.

> *"Let all that you do be done in love."*
>
> **—1 CORINTHIANS 16:14** NASB

7

Jim, Lisa, and Paul

Jim and Lisa are in grief. They discovered their three-year-old son, Paul, had a cancerous tumor attached to his spine. They went through about three months of various treatments to try to eradicate the tumor.

There were weeks of ups and downs—tests that showed the tumor shrinking and then days when Paul couldn't feel or move his legs. Jim and Lisa kept holding out hope that he would be healed.

Then things took a rapid turn for the worst. Doctors found a tumor in Paul's brain. It was inoperable and growing rapidly. The doctors said there was no cure. Within a week, little Paul was with Jesus.

During the whole ordeal, Jim sent out email messages to update family and friends and to request prayer. We certainly don't want to exploit this tragedy or belittle this family's loss, but a few excerpts from those emails are worth repeating. Once in a while, we all need a wake-up call.

During those last days, Jim wrote, "We are doing all we can to make Paul comfortable and ready for a glorified body, with working legs to run and play with the other kids with Jesus."

Then, after his son had died, here's what Jim wrote: "Lisa and I held him in our arms as we talked to him and to God about being ready. It was a peaceful passing."

Now, we have two challenges for you, Dad. First, what worries and challenges are you facing today? This family's trials remind us that from an eternal perspective, our daily stresses aren't all that significant. We have much to be thankful for, and our children are right at the top of that list.

Second, imagine holding your child in your arms and preparing him to meet Jesus. It's an incredible thought! But in a very real sense, that's exactly what fathers do. Yes, we're preparing them to achieve great things here on earth. Things that bring personal satisfaction and give glory to God. In the moment, we're helping them discern and harvest their gifts and talents. But let's never forget, this world is a finger snap compared to eternity.

The story of Jim, Lisa, and Paul touches us because of the order of events. When we begin a family, we expect our children to outlive us. But sometimes it doesn't work out that way. Either way, the truth remains. Our children will leave this world someday. They will meet Jesus.

No matter what, we should feel an urgency, just as Paul's daddy did. Our number one job is to prepare our kids for eternity.

From a purely human perspective, death is tragic and often unexplainable. But for those of us who trust in Jesus, death is a victory, a coming home. We have the awesome responsibility of passing that hope and that destiny to our children.

What's more, we don't think it's selfish to look forward to that time when loved ones are reunited in heaven. Would you agree?

> *"Jesus answered him, 'Truly I tell you, today you will be with me in paradise.'"*
>
> **—LUKE 23:43**

★ ★ ★

8

Be Yourself

Hey, Dad, do you have a fashion or lifestyle statement that's uniquely you?

Maybe cowboy boots? Or a super-hip fedora? Black socks with shorts? Playing blues on the harmonica? Making s'mores with saltines? Cooking rattlesnake on the grill?

What's your unique contribution, Dad? The men of the National Center for Fathering are officially giving you a thumbs-up, a high five, and a manly head nod from across the room. In other words, let your flag fly. How you present yourself to the world is very probably 99 percent awesome—and wonderfully valuable as you seek to be a reliable model for your kids.

The Bible teaches that even though some things are black and white, God gives us a lot of room for self-expression. That's not to say we should be purposefully sinful, selfish, or offensive. But living a little off the wall is perfectly fine. Even John the Baptist wore a camel-hair coat and ate locusts and honey.

Your unique style may even help your kids deal with peer pressure. Watching you—even when they roll their eyes—they are learning to think for themselves.

When a dad breaks out of the mold as an individual—not just for the sake of being different, but when he's being himself—consider how that impacts his kids. Not to worry. Your kids will probably not start dressing like you or grooving to the oldies radio station. Those

29

personality or style quirks may be a running joke in the family for years to come. But beneath the joking, kids recognize that Dad has the courage to be himself—even when no one else joins him.

Our children are watching us, and if we're conforming to someone else's image, then we're probably teaching our children to do the same. So again, one of our jobs is to teach them to value their own uniqueness. They need to realize that life is going to give them choices to make. Some of those choices give glory to God. Many have no moral implications. But others are hurtful, evil, and destructive.

A little biblical guidance from Dad may be in order. Good advice such as 1 Corinthians 15:33. "Do not be misled: 'Bad company corrupts good character.'"

As they get older, help your children also to understand they have a responsibility to their friends and siblings. They could make bad decisions that have a negative impact on others. Open your Bible to Romans 14:13 and read it out loud: "Make up your mind not to put any stumbling block or obstacle in the way of a brother or sister."

Dad, while you're preparing those snippets of Scripture for your kids, make sure you apply them to your own personal style and choices. If you're hanging out with "bad company" and allowing your character to be corrupted, there's a good chance you may be causing those kids you love so much to stumble.

You wouldn't let that happen to them, would you?

On the other hand, when a dad combs his hair in a ducktail or shaves his head or keeps his 25-year-old mullet, he may embarrass his kids, but he's not dishonoring the kingdom.

You might even say he's teaching his kids that self-expression is okay—*if* it doesn't dishonor God.

So be yourself, Dad. Give your kids a living example of a man who thinks for himself and celebrates the way God has created him.

Then hope, pray, and expect your kids do the same.

"Dads have a responsibility to embarrass their teenager once in a while, but the goal is to get eye rolls and mild exasperated groans, not screams of agony as your child runs from the room. Make sure you know the difference."

—CAREY CASEY

9

Anger and Priorities

Clint comes home from work, and young Mark and Grace give him a joyous welcome. They've been waiting all afternoon to go outside and play with Dad. Clint shakes them loose from his arms and legs for a minute so he can change clothes, and he takes the mail upstairs with him.

His five-year-old son follows, talking about what happened that day, overflowing with comments that draw from both reality and make-believe. It's too much for Clint to follow. "Mark," he says, "can't you see I'm trying to read the mail? Let's talk about this later."

Back downstairs, Clint's wife is nowhere to be found. And that's fine—after an entire day with the kids, she needs to get away. So Clint fixes a plate of leftovers and clicks on the TV. On cue, two-year-old Grace approaches, wanting handouts. Soon Mark enters the room. "Can we go play outside now, Daddy?"

Little Grace hears the word "outside" and excitedly runs to look for her shoes. "Pretty soon, son," Clint answers. As he eats, Clint gets involved in a news bulletin that relates to his work. The instant Mark sees his dad put his last forkful of leftovers into his mouth, the boy asks, "Now, Daddy?" Clint's voice begins to show his impatience: "What did I tell you? We'll do it in a little while." His eyes dart back to the TV.

Now Mark starts whining—despite his father's admonitions to talk calmly. Grace returns with her shoes on the wrong feet and joins the chorus. Mark's pleas get more and more desperate, leading to an all-out tantrum: "But, Daddy, you said we could go outside! When?"

Now Clint is frustrated and angry about missing a soundbite from the news report. "I don't want to hear another word about it," he says. "I said we would go outside. Just be patient!"

Clint did take them outside several minutes later, but the tone for the evening was already set. He was overly critical and short with them, and any wrong move brought more threats and harsh words. Their "fun time" outside was anything but fun.

Now, let's step back for a minute. Our research reveals that fathers' struggle with anger is undeniably common. Every dad is unique, but we think many dads can identify with Clint's experience. He's a good dad, but he let himself get off track and spiral out of control.

Why does it happen?

The Bible says, "What causes fights and quarrels among you? Don't they come from your desires that battle within you?" (James 4:1). So often, frustration and anger start as an inner conflict between priorities. We want to do one thing, but family responsibilities pull us another way. During that battle between what we *want* to do and what we know we *should* do, the negative emotions continue to grow.

In the example, Clint expressed his negative emotions as threats and harsh words. If a dad doesn't recognize his error and commit to change, the bad habits will escalate. Being short with a daughter could lead to cruel, demeaning statements, screaming at her for little mistakes, or even physical abuse.

Children will misbehave. They will disobey. They will whine and throw fits...but they do not cause their father's response. And that's the point. We are responsible for how we respond. We're the adults. We need to establish and honor the priorities of the moment.

Responding calmly to our children begins with asking God for an ever-present awareness of his priorities for our lives. With that in place, there's no inner conflict and much less likelihood of negative emotions when relating to our kids. The decision has already been made: We're going to do what's best for them.

How do you make this happen? During moments of clarity—when you feel conviction about making changes in your life or becoming a better dad—write down your thoughts or make a mental note about how you'll live out your priority and commitment.

When do you tend to get angry with your kids? What actions can you commit to that will make a difference? Maybe, like Clint, you need a specific plan that will help you transition more smoothly from work to home. Or maybe it means turning off distractions, such as the TV or computer. Or asking your wife for help.

Dads, we'll never be perfect or always under control. But with God's help and a real desire to change, we can truly have our priorities in order. Matthew 6:33 is still very much in effect—"Seek first his kingdom and his righteousness." Then, remember that your first ministry is to your family.

> *"When you're home, Dad, make sure you're really home."*
>
> **—BROCK GRIFFIN**

★ ★ ★

10

Don't Be a Loaf of Bread

For some dads, the best advice you'll receive between the covers of this book is this: Don't be a loaf of bread. Confused? Read on, friend.

In the early Proverbs, much of the wisdom Solomon dispenses is from father to son. There are sections warning against folly, extolling the benefits of wisdom, and warning against adultery and other temptations.

Chapter 6 provides a clear warning against an adulteress woman: "Do not desire her beauty in your heart, nor let her capture you with her eyelids. For on account of a harlot one is reduced to a loaf of bread, and an adulteress hunts for the precious life" (Proverbs 6:25-26 NASB).

A loaf of bread! Who'd want to be described like that?

Well, that's any man who's not careful. Without digging too deep into your imagination, you know exactly what this "adulterous woman" looks like and the temptations she radiates. The above passage spells it out. She has desirable beauty and fluttering eyelashes, and she's on the hunt for a man who has let down his guard. What she promises is wrapped in a package you might even be tempted to buy for a few crusts of bread. But don't do it! Otherwise, the value of your own life is reduced to that same paltry sum.

The temptation to lust is ever present. But without minimizing the dangers of pornography and other forms of sexual immorality, let's look beyond the fear of being seduced by an adulterous woman.

There's an even larger trend impacting dads, luring them from their families and reducing them to bread crumbs.

Too many dads are squandering time on leisure pursuits. They're piddling around on things that don't really matter while important opportunities with their wives and children and in their churches are passing by. They're enthralled by the latest video downloads or social media craze. Computer games, extreme sports, fantasy leagues, golf, tennis, ironman triathlons, managing stocks, restoring classic cars, and woodworking get their best passion and energy. They're dawdling in front of the computer or not getting enough sleep because they're up late watching television or researching the next big trend.

Like the adulterous woman, hobbies and frivolous pursuits are "capturing" dads for long periods of time and distracting them from what God wants them to be doing—engaging in prayer and study, reaching out to the widow and the fatherless, and building strong bonds with their wives and children. Men are being seduced by selfishness and amusement, and they're gradually becoming loaves of bread.

We understand how it happens. It's tough to stay focused with all the influences in our culture. We give in just a little bit every day, and before we know it, we're way off course.

For sure, hobbies can be good things. They can help you relax and take your mind off some of the frustrations of life. Sometimes they can even evolve into connecting points with your family. Heading into your workshop to build a pair of stilts with a nine-year-old. Golfing with your bride. Hobbies may even open up opportunities for evangelism with clubs like Bikers for Jesus or church basketball leagues.

But, Dad, we hope you hear this message. Allow yourself to be lured, coaxed, and enticed into a closer relationship with your family. We're setting the tone in our homes, showing our children what it means to be a husband, father, and man. We need to wake up and realize how precious those opportunities are.

Don't be a loaf of bread. Don't be a bump on a log. Don't squander your best self. Be a man of substance and virtue. Make sure you're investing yourself in things that have eternal significance.

"The best way to prevent yourself from being burned by temptation is to take an intentional step back from the flame."

—JAY PAYLEITNER

Comforting Childhood Fears

During Jared's first week of kindergarten, he started asking his parents some probing questions. "Will I get lost at school?" "Will someone come and try to take me?" Even, "What will happen to me if you die?"

It was a big time of adjustment. Everything and everyone at the school were new for Jared. As he tried to figure out where he fit in, some deep questions surfaced.

At first, Jared's parents tried to answer his questions logically. They told him, "Many teachers and your principal are watching over you." They even talked about who was prepared to take care of him if neither of them could.

Then it occurred to Jared's dad that those answers were insufficient. Jared's fears were based on legitimate questions. Really, when it came down to it, he couldn't completely guarantee Jared's safety. Only one Father could do that.

So Jared's dad started talking to his son about how they trust God to take care of them. He gave a few examples of minor mishaps from family history as proof that things work out in the long run. Talking to his son in a calm and confident tone, he used words like "trust" and "faith" and "love." It turns out that even a five-year-old boy can grasp the idea that in this world some hard things might happen, but we can trust God to bring about good things and receive glory even through those tough times.

Then this wise father opened the family Bible. He read to his son from Psalm 46: "God is our refuge and strength, an ever-present help in trouble. Therefore we will not fear." He read from Hebrews 13, where the writer quotes God's assurances in Deuteronomy and Psalms: "Never will I leave you; never will I forsake you...The Lord is my helper; I will not be afraid."

Turning to Scripture is the obvious choice if we really believe Hebrews 4:12, which promises, "The word of God is alive and active." It has supernatural power to comfort our children, and we should all use it for that purpose. Because in many ways, the childlike fears never end. A young boy might fear the unknown, a teenager might be afraid of being rejected, and let's face it, we grown-ups still have our share of fears and concerns.

Dad, we need to claim God's comfort for our family through his Word—and do it often. Then take it a step further and let your daily life show that God is our ever-present help in time of need and that we depend on Him for everything.

> *"With a Father in heaven and a father to tuck them in at night, a child's fears should just about disappear."*
>
> **—CAREY CASEY**

★ ★ ★

12

The Case of the Submerged Cell Phone

Pastor Rick was camping with his family at the lake, taking some well-deserved vacation time. One morning, as they were getting ready to go fishing, Rick walked along the dock toward the boat with his arms full of gear, stumbled on a loose board, and lost his balance. As he was flailing around to avoid falling in the water, his cell phone popped from his pocket and plopped into the lake.

For a good half-hour, Rick and other family members dove in to find his phone, but it was no use. They finally gave up and went on with the day's plans. Rick tried to put it behind him and have a good time, but he couldn't relax—he just couldn't get over losing his cell phone like that.

You can probably guess what happened that night as Rick was getting the kids ready for bed. His ten-year-old son said, "Dad, I'm sure glad you lost your phone today."

Rick was shocked. "Why, son?"

"Because if you hadn't, you would have been looking at it all day."

Rick's first thought was, *That isn't true.* He just needed to be available if someone needed him or if something urgent came up at the church. But then he realized the deeper message. Whether it was true or not, Rick's son perceived that sometimes his father's cell phone and work responsibilities were more important than he was. Ouch.

There are all kinds of lessons here, but let's camp on just two.

First, sometimes we have to put aside the urgent in favor of what's most important. We can easily get into the habit of letting our smartphones or our work schedules rule our lives—at the expense of investing in our families. Taking a deliberate time-out or vacation from electronic media is something we need to do for ourselves and to demonstrate to our children that it can be done.

And second, we need to remember the importance of focused attention. Of course, Rick cares more about his son than his job. But the boy didn't know that! Said another way, the time we spend with our kids needs to be spent *with our kids*.

We've trained ourselves to multitask so we can get more done every day. That's great at work, but it isn't usually a good idea at home. Do you ever catch yourself asking your daughter about her day while scanning your smartphone or tablet...and eating dinner...with the evening news on?

Dad, don't wait until your cell phone is at the bottom of a lake. Make sure your kids know they are a priority in your life today. And prove it with regular doses of undivided, unplugged, and uninterrupted attention.

"The best gift a father can give to a child is himself."

JAY PAYLEITNER

13

Stretching to Connect

We know dads who have attended ballet classes with their daughters. They actually practiced and then performed with them at the recital. We know dads who have downloaded jump-rope videos and memorized sequences to help their daughters develop new maneuvers for competition. We also know dads who never learned to play chess, but when their middle-schooler showed an interest, these men studied the game just so they could spend a little extra time with their growing son or daughter.

Getting involved in your children's world is an important way to communicate your love. It also gives you new opportunities to learn more about your children and what makes them tick. It's stepping out of your comfort zone, trying to view the world from your child's perspective, and finding that point of connection. That's especially true for daughters. Often fathers can relate to their sons but have to stretch to see the world through the eyes of their little girl.

This idea of stretching yourself to connect with your kids can open up new worlds to explore with them.

If they show a spark of promise in some area, lead the cheers when they suddenly pass you up in knowledge or ability. You might even ask them to teach you a thing or two. If you can humble yourself and allow them to take the lead, you'll probably deliver a nice boost to their self-confidence.

If you see an area in which they have a weakness or vulnerability, you might want to become a student yourself, learning strategies and developing new skills right along with them. Suddenly you're a team, sharing frustrations and celebrating breakthroughs.

One great idea is to talk with your children's mother about how you can help prepare each of your kids for issues or challenges they'll face in the next six or twelve months. Or ask your children what part of *your* world they'd like to learn more about and arrange to let them join you in that.

Men, we believe connecting with your kids on their terms is critical to your relationship. You can make this happen at any stage of your children's lives.

If you have an infant, dive in and become an expert at feeding, changing, burping, cleaning up, and so on. Be easy on yourself if you aren't a natural right from the start. Taking care of your baby is one of the best ways to bond.

With preschoolers, get down on their level and follow their lead. Participate in whatever they're doing, even if you think it might look silly to be huddling around a tiny table for a tea party or dancing and singing in public. Also, be willing to play the same game, read the same book, or do the same puzzle over and over again.

School-age kids are involved in a hundred different things. Keeping up with your kids' ballet rehearsals, karate lessons, art classes…this may require a real stretch or sacrifice of your time. Be especially aware of the latest games, toys, and gimmicks.

For teens, you may have to work your schedule around theirs. Keep up with the sports and hobbies they enjoy, music they listen to, and technology they use. Maintaining routines (especially meals together), supporting their school activities, and attending church as a family are vitally important.

When your children are young adults, they truly do have their own lives. More than ever, connecting with them means going to where they are and being part of what they're doing. Try spending a night at the college dorm and sitting in on a class or two or getting involved in a project at their workplace or in their community.

Finally, many of these suggestions apply when grandkids come along. Grandfathers can and should make themselves available to give their children a break from their kids sometimes—for an evening, a few days, or a week—so those young parents can get away, refresh and recharge, and strengthen their marriage.

You can see how intentionally connecting with your children is a lifelong and rewarding goal. Each season of life builds on the one before. The more you are involved with younger kids, the better chance you have to stay engaged all the way through their adult lives. But no matter what, you can still stretch yourself and get involved in the sweet spot of life your kids are in right now. Don't miss it, Dad.

> *"One of the most important skills today's father needs is the ability to step out of his comfort zone."*
>
> **—BROCK GRIFFIN**

★ ★ ★

14

Indispensable Dads

Your daughter's second-grade school program is scheduled in the middle of a workday. She's playing a lion and has no speaking lines. The play only lasts 20 minutes, but the drive from your office is at least a half hour each way.

What do you do? Do you add that complication to your schedule and race back and forth to the school? Or do you excuse yourself and tell your daughter you'll make the next one, when she has a bigger role?

It's a classic work-family dilemma. We want to support our kids, but our jobs are important too. They help define who we are as men.

A dad named Mark wrestled frequently with that kind of work-family dilemma. We interviewed him as part of our Father of the Year contest, and we want to share one of his insights.

He said, "When we're at work, we like to feel important and vital to the company. We show how important we are by staying busy. We position ourselves to give the impression that we have a lot to do, and we can't possibly break away unless it's really important." Mark finished that insight with this zinger: "We like to think we are more indispensable at work than we really are."

That thought forces each of us to ask another question: Are you indispensable at work? What would happen if you left your job tomorrow? Sure, it might be a big hassle for everyone, but in a few weeks or a month, they would bring in someone else to replace you. They'd miss you for a while, but there are probably a number of people who have the skills to replace you in your job. The company or organization would go on.

Now, think about this: What if you died tomorrow? Who could your family find to replace you at home? *Nobody.* You can never be replaced. The loss would be immeasurable. To your family, Dad, you are indispensable.

Taking a step back, the ongoing struggle of the work-family dilemma shouldn't be minimized. Men can't quit their jobs just to attend a second-grade school program. Mark shouldn't be burdened with guilt if unavoidable commitments keep him at work. But all dads should continue to ask themselves, *Where am I most indispensable?*

Keep that thought in mind the next time a child has a game, a performance, or some other event. You can be sure your son or daughter is looking out in the seats for support and encouragement. They know you have other responsibilities. They may not know exactly what you do for a living, but they know other people are counting on you. Still, they're scanning the crowd for the man they call Daddy.

We'd love to let you off the hook and say that in the long run, it doesn't really matter. But you know what? It does matter. So if at all possible, be there. This is not a guilt trip. Or an ultimatum. It's a fact.

Dad, *no one* and *nothing* can take your place. And that's a good thing. When it comes right down to it, at home we proudly wear the title "Indispensable."

> "In the NFL, players on the sidelines look into the camera and say, 'Hi, Mom!' But when they look into the stands, they're looking for their dad."
>
> **—CAREY CASEY**

15

Sensitive, Supportive, Challenging

How you engage with your toddlers today will impact how you interact with them during their teen years.

A study completed several years ago at the University of Regensburg, Germany, may help you lay the groundwork for building a father-child relationship that's closer than you can imagine. The researchers even provided three helpful words that you'll want to take to heart: Sensitive. Supportive. Challenging.

Now, you might be the kind of dad who already recognizes the benefits of those three characteristics. On the other hand, you might be hearing this idea for the first time. Either way, the idea is not so much to know it, but to put it into practice.

The 16-year study assessed how men interacted with their children at ages two, ten, and sixteen. Researchers gave high scores to fathers who talked to their toddlers in an age-appropriate way, stimulated and encouraged their children, made appealing suggestions for play, and refrained from criticism. Worth noting, the quality of the dads' play was found to be comparable to the strength of the mother-infant bond in predicting children's ability to form enduring relationships later in life.

Now, those three words—sensitive, supportive, and challenging—are strikingly similar to Paul's description of a father's role in 1 Thessalonians 2:11-12: "You know that we dealt with each of you as a father deals with his own children, encouraging, comforting and urging you to live lives worthy of God, who calls you into his kingdom and glory."

Those words, "encouraging, comforting and urging," provide a critical reminder that as dads, we have great power to build up our kids or tear them down.

Being sensitive, supportive, and challenging is a good description of a key virtue we encourage fathers to develop—gentleness. Gentleness as a father begins with maintaining composure through the highs and lows that come with having young children. As Proverbs 15:1 says, "A gentle answer turns away wrath."

Gentleness also leads us to being more proactive than reactive. A reactive dad might fly off the handle when one of his children messes up, defies him, interrupts, or makes one more request of his time. A reactive dad is likely to act impulsively in response to the urgent issues pressing on him—which aren't usually the most important matters in the long run.

But a proactive dad chooses how to act based on predetermined priorities and principles. He maintains an awareness that his relationships with his children are more important than most other demands, and he responds to his children's requests with calmness. A proactive dad sees the long-term big picture and is approachable and slow to anger. He seldom overreacts, even when correcting or disciplining his children.

Make it your goal to be a gentle dad. Learning to be sensitive, supportive, and challenging—those three words again—with your children during their early years will serve you well when your children grow into teenagers and young adults.

> *"It shouldn't be a surprise when researchers invest many hours uncovering a new insight, only to realize it's already clearly stated in God's Word."*
>
> **—BROCK GRIFFIN**

★ ★ ★

16

Manna for Fathers

One Saturday, Brad and his four-year-old son, Davy, rode their bikes to the park. But after only a few minutes of playing, Davy scrunched up his nose and called to his dad, "I gotta go."

There were no bathrooms around, so Brad told him, "That's fine. We just have to ride back home." Of course, Davy didn't want to leave, so he said, "I can hold it." Like many fathers in that same situation, Brad made a big mistake—he believed his son.

A few minutes later, Davy was scrunching up his nose again and kind of reaching around toward his backside. "I gotta go, Daddy!" This time he meant business, so Brad ran over. "Okay," he said, "let's hurry home."

But this was an emergency, and little Davy was trying to take down his britches right there on the walkway between the slide and the monkey bars. Brad grabbed Davy to stop him. "You can't do it here," he said.

So the pants stayed up, but Brad now had a sad, embarrassed four-year-old and a mess to deal with. They couldn't exactly get back on the bikes like this.

Brad carried Davy away from the other kids and parents and set him down. How could he possibly handle this? As he took a deep breath, his eyes wandered over to a big tree not far from the playground. And wouldn't you know it? Someone had thrown toilet paper in the tree the night before. And it had rained after that, so there were white clumps of toilet paper strewn across the ground…like manna. It's a true story with a happy ending.

With a little covert activity, Brad was able to get Davy cleaned up and back on the bike, and they headed home.

Now, we don't want to make too much of this lighthearted story except to offer this reminder: God is there for us as fathers. He's there for the daily messes and the big, earth-shattering problems. He knows just what we need for every situation, whether it's a word of advice or encouragement from another dad, a Sunday sermon that speaks to your need and provides hope, a wife who provides her insights and support, or something totally unexpected.

Sometimes all we need to do is stop for a second, take a deep breath, say a prayer, and look around for the manna.

"If you've never been surprised by God's provision, maybe you're still trying to do life without his help."

—CAREY CASEY

17

The Key to Your Daughter's Heart

Anyone who visits the National Center for Fathering should expect that at some point, the conversation will focus on fatherhood. Because that's who we are, and that's what we do.

Not long ago, we were talking with a bright young lady about her relationship with her father, and one statement stood out: "All I know about my dad is that he is in a suit and he's successful."

This daughter clearly perceives that her dad has it all together, but their relationship doesn't go much deeper than the surface. She really doesn't know him well. She probably doesn't know what drives him, what worries him, what he values most, what his goals are, or what she really means to him.

Sadly, that kind of distant father-daughter relationship is not unusual in today's fast-paced, disconnected culture.

Another father, Joe, and his daughter had a similar relationship…until they attended a father-daughter event sponsored by NCF in Texas. Joe sent us a long email about his experience. Here's a portion:

> One major eye-opener for me happened during the lunch break. While we were apart, we were instructed to write our daughters a letter. I wrote about how she is beautiful, smart, talented, and a blessing to me. I filled the whole card! My daughter was excited to read it. When I saw her again, she had a card for me! Here's what it said:
>
> "Dad, thank you for making me be here cuz I have

learned a lot. And now I feel like I can talk to you about anything. I am looking forward to doing something together again—maybe next weekend. I just want to say I love you and thank you for being there for me."

I cried. I simply cried. I'll never lose the card I received from my daughter or let anything happen to it. It's very special to me because it came from someone very special.

It's pretty clear that an intentional weekend away had a powerful impact on Joe's relationship with his daughter. And we need to give him much of the credit. Joe took several proactive positive steps. He researched the event. He insisted his daughter attend. He wasn't afraid to be honest and real when he wrote a card to his daughter. And when he received her response, he let the emotion of the moment touch his heart. Well done, Joe.

NCF also sponsors essay contests for schoolchildren around the country. One girl wrote, "My dad holds the key to the unlocked door of my heart."

Men, it's time to move out of our comfort zone—especially with our daughters. We need to be their daddy and make sure they see more than our work persona. We need to humble ourselves, making sure they know how much we love them and going overboard with words of affirmation. And we need to realize the power we have to unlock the door of their heart.

A sticky note. A long letter. A quiet conversation. A dinner for two. A bike ride to Dairy Queen. Or maybe even a weekend away. What can you do in the next few days to help build a bond of mutual love, respect, and admiration with your wonderful, fabulous daughter?

"When a father opens his heart to his children, he is giving them permission and freedom to open their hearts to him."

—BROCK GRIFFIN

★ ★ ★

18

The Grass Will Come Back

A man named Kevin tells this story about his father. The event took place when Kevin was 12 years old, though Kevin didn't hear about it until many years later.

Their family lived on a 26-acre farm, and there weren't any kids around who were Kevin's age, so he found ways to entertain himself. Kevin's dad did his son a favor by buying him a little Yamaha dirt bike, which provided him with many hours of fun.

You know how 12-year-old boys are. Even with all that space, Kevin's riding track just had to include the front and back lawn next to the house. Round and round he would go, living out childhood adventures of chasing bad guys or winning races. It didn't take long for him to carve a nice little dirt track through the grass, around the house, and back out into the pasture.

One day a neighbor finally asked Kevin's dad the obvious and logical question. (You were thinking it too, right?) He asked, "How come you let your son tear up the yard like that? Why don't you make him ride that thing out in the pasture?"

Kevin's dad was a man of few words but uncommon wisdom. He said to the neighbor, "The grass will come back, but the boy won't."

Maybe someone has asked you that question about the two bare spots where you and your son play catch, or the ruts beneath the swing set. Or maybe there's some sign of wear and tear inside your house that shows your kids' activity.

We may be walking a fine line here because we don't want our children to be completely careless or to disregard our property. They do need to learn respect and responsibility. But as dads, let's pledge to make sure we let our kids be kids.

Encourage them to express their imagination and exuberance—even if it stretches normal boundaries a little bit. Give them freedom to take risks while they're under your watchful eye.

Your teenage daughter wants to paint her room purple? Buy the paint, put down a drop cloth, demonstrate proper painting technique, and then get out of her way.

Your son and his friends dent your garage door playing driveway stickball? At least they weren't playing some creepy, dark video game.

Your kitchen table has a spattering of spots from a chemistry project that got out of hand? Congratulations! You may be raising a chemical engineer who someday wins a Nobel Prize.

Encouraging their freedom reflects your commitment to your children and your desire to see them grow and develop with a sense of adventure and confidence.

It's like Kevin's dad said—the grass or the bushes will grow back. The bedroom can be repainted. The garage door can be replaced. The kitchen table can be refinished.

Then again, you may want to leave all those imperfections exactly as they are. Every time you look at that lawn, room, door, table, or whatever, you can remember that season of life when you let your kid be a kid.

> *"The childhood years are short and precious.*
> *Help your child find ways to enjoy them for all*
> *they're worth, and you'll enjoy them too."*
>
> **—CAREY CASEY**

★ ★ ★

19

Talking *with* Your Kids, Not *at* Them

A not-so-funny joke…

One evening your fourth grader walks into the house after an event at school. "Hey, Dad," he says, "I can't believe it! I got a part in the school play."

"Great," you say, barely looking up from your smartphone. "What part did you get?"

"I'm the dad," he says.

From the other room, your wife says, "That's okay, Johnny. Maybe next time you'll get a speaking part."

Not laughing? Well, in theory, the reason it's funny is because it contains a nugget of truth. Quite a few dads have earned a reputation of being noncommunicative. When they do speak, they talk *at* the kids and not *with* them. Or they might attempt to hold a conversation, but they do more lecturing than listening.

Conversing with our children benefits us and our kids. It's pretty high on the list of fathering priorities. So let's consider a few strategies for strengthening your verbal interaction skills with those kids you love so much.

One idea is to speak blessings to your children. Even if you already tell them you love them, it's valuable to express your commitment and appreciation in other ways. Look your son or daughter squarely in the eye and give them a word gift.

"I'm proud of you."

"It's a privilege just to be your dad."

"When I see you make time for your little sister, it blesses me."

"A guy at work was telling me about how his teenage son is getting into so much trouble. And I just want to say thank you for who you are."

"I was thinking about you today. And the way God has gifted you. I can't wait to see how he continues to work in your life to do great things...no pressure!"

Your words of blessing can stand on their own when you and your child happen to be in the same room, or they could launch a conversation. Either way, try to point out positives to your children whenever you can. Be specific. Don't make stuff up because kids can smell a load of baloney a kilometer away.

Another way to engage your children in conversation is to ask questions. Not as an interrogation, but just to relate. Your questions let them know you care. Steer clear of the obvious clichés. "How was school today?" "How was rehearsal?" The response to those kinds of questions is usually that classic one-word answer: "Fine." You're more likely to start an actual conversation if you already know a little about what's going on in their lives. "When you start dissecting frogs in biology, how many kids per frog?" "How can you rehearse the balcony scene before the set is even built?"

In the same way, you may not get much of a response if you ask, "What are your hopes and dreams?" Instead try questions like, "If you could live in any state or country for five years, where would that be?" "I know it's a few years away, but do you think you'd like to go to a small college or a big university?" "What's the toughest thing going on in your life right now?"

If all else fails, ask their opinions on current news events. Don't be surprised if they're better informed than you think. And also don't be surprised if their politics or worldview is a little different from yours.

Don't belittle or judge too harshly. They're still taking it all in and forming their opinions.

No matter what, when the conversation is over, make sure they're glad they spent that time with you.

Men, we need to become experts in the art of having verbal interaction with our children. It may not come easy. You may have to overcome years of bad habits. But caring, thoughtful conversations are really the best way to fill the silence and fill their hearts.

> *"One of the best ways to get your kids talking is to tell them about the ups and downs of your own day. And even ask for their advice."*
>
> **—JAY PAYLEITNER**

★ ★ ★

20

Knee Prints in the Carpet

As fathers, we're powerful models. Our words and actions are constantly being monitored by those little ones we love so much. That includes the books we read and the television shows we watch. Table manners, driving habits, and the way we respect their mother. Whether we use our mouths to bless or curse. They are watching, and they see it all.

Perhaps the most important habit we can model for our children is how we interact with the Creator of the universe. Is it only with short, obligatory prayers at mealtime? Or do we engage in thoughtful prayers of thanks and praise throughout the day?

Recently, we heard about a college-age girl who was home from school one weekend and having a conversation with her mother. "Mom," she said, "I really draw great comfort from knowing that you and Dad still pray for me all the time."

The mother acknowledged, "Yeah, we sure do, honey. We still pray for you every day."

But to the daughter, this was more than just a passing comment. She said, "No, you still pray just like when I was home—at least I know Daddy does."

Now she really had her mother's curiosity going. "What do you mean?"

The daughter said, "In my bedroom…I can see the knee marks on the carpet where Daddy kneels next to my bed—exactly how he used to pray for me at bedtime."

The surprised mother acknowledged that he does still do that, and the daughter said, "You know, when I'm away at school, I can picture him kneeling down in my room, and it makes me feel like everything is going to be okay."

That image of a dad on his knees lifting up his daughter in prayer should be a motivation for all of us. Couldn't we all be more disciplined about praying daily for each of our children? Might we do better at assuming a physical posture that demonstrates our submission to God's will as we ask for his guidance, protection, and blessing? We don't want to be legalistic about prayer. God wants us to seek him anytime and anyplace. As 1 Thessalonians 5:17 says, we should "pray continually." Still, maybe it's time we got off our rear ends and got down on our knees.

When we pray, invisible forces surround our family and each of our children. Prayer is believing that what is unseen can actually become a reality because we have a Father who is unseen and who hears the cries of our hearts.

Whether or not we see our kids every day, and whether or not we can kneel beside their beds, we all need to pray faithfully, specifically, intensely, and daily for our children.

If we really want to make a difference for our families, the best place to start and end our days is on our knees.

> "When you pray, go into your room, close the door and pray to your Father, who is unseen. Then your Father, who sees what is done in secret, will reward you."
>
> **—MATTHEW 6:6**

21

$1.77

Because of who we are and what we stand for, we get some unusual mail at the National Center for Fathering.

Some time ago, we heard from a young girl who expressed a need that revealed a spiritual maturity well beyond her years. She sent us this letter, written in her own longhand, and titled it "Prayer Request."

> I pray in Jesus' name that Dad and I would be able to talk to each other without any hurtful words being spoken. I claim for my family that God would make Daddy a good spiritual leader, and make him who God wants him to be. In Jesus' name, amen.

It's a heartfelt sentiment, and we can only imagine the environment in which that little girl is growing up. Reading between the lines of her letter, it seems that her daddy may be lashing out on occasion with harsh words and emotions. But we don't know that. Perhaps she has seen anger unleashed in other homes and is wisely asking for God's protection on her family.

We do know one thing. This little girl is clear on the concept that it's a father's job to be the spiritual leader in the home.

But the real kicker is what she included along with the letter—a money order to the National Center for Fathering in the amount of one dollar and seventy-seven cents. We suspect that a dollar seventy-seven may have been all she had after shaking her piggy bank for every last penny.

We gather regularly at the NCF for prayer. This prayer request got our full attention for several of those daily gatherings. We believe those collective prayers also moved the heart of God.

The other interesting thing about her letter is the way she connected spiritual leadership with the ability to talk to each other in a respectful way. Respect and communication are key elements of leading our children to Christ. They need to see evidence in our lives that we really do love the Lord with all our heart, soul, mind, and strength.

That all comes out in the way we treat people—especially our children. Our walk with Christ should be obvious and attractive to our kids. If we can't make our faith look like a rewarding and joy-filled journey, why would our kids want any part of it?

So please remember, Dad, that spiritual equipping does matter to your kids. This little girl probably gave all the money she had in a desperate hope that we could somehow help her dad be the leader she needs him to be. But in sending her last pennies, maybe what she's really saying is, a godly father is worth everything we have.

We can't possibly put a price tag on the value of a man providing a spiritual foundation for his family. All we can do is ask, *what are you willing to invest?*

> *"If you want to know your children's deepest needs, all you really have to do is listen. To their heart. To your heart. To God's heart."*
>
> **—CAREY CASEY**

22

The Joy and Rewards of Work

Do you ever find yourself thinking this? *Kids these days are just lazy. They just sit around all day watching TV and playing video games.*

Well, Dad, maybe you can do something about that. A dad named Robin sent in an idea he uses to train his 11-year-old son, Scott, to be a responsible and well-rounded young man.

Robin says he looks for ways to teach his son how to work, the rewards of work, and the joy of work. It started with chores around the house but soon expanded to include various work activities and projects with other adults, including relatives, friends from work or church, or neighbors.

Robin said the initiative really came together when he began to look for work opportunities for his son that would provide two specific benefits—learning new skills and feeling the satisfaction of having completed a job well done.

Over time, Scott learned such skills as milking a cow, painting buildings, creating art, gardening, carpentry, and splitting firewood.

Robin warns other dads that the process takes more time and effort than you may expect. He spent more than a few hours researching projects for his son and making sure each job would be a positive experience. Taking an 11-year-old on a work project and taking the time to teach and explain things will most likely slow things down. But it's worth the effort.

Robin's son is learning skills of lifelong value. Kids in Scott's stage of life need to be exposed to many different things as they explore their place in the world. In addition, these times together help keep the father-son relationship strong. Not to mention, Scott gets to rub shoulders with other men who are strong role models.

Maybe the biggest benefit is that now, after all these great experiences, Scott has a positive attitude about work. He jumps at the chance to get involved, and he sees each new project as an adventure, not a chore.

Dad, a healthy attitude toward work gives your children a huge advantage in their studies, in their careers, in their marriages, and in their service to God and people.

It may take a little time and effort, but isn't preparing your kids for life pretty much your job description as a dad? Your kids are counting on you to help them experience the joy and rewards of work.

> *"Good planning and hard work lead to prosperity,*
> *but hasty shortcuts lead to poverty."*
>
> **—PROVERBS 21:5 NLT**

★ ★ ★

23

Fathering with Purpose

This chapter may or may not be worth reading. It may or may not have some valuable advice for dads.

An hour or so of clacking on a keyboard without any real preparation or thoughtful plan is probably not going to make our editors happy or be worthy of your time, but we're hopeful it might be. We're actually not even sure where this chapter will end, because we're just winging it. Lord willing, some wisdom may leap out from the page, but you probably shouldn't count on it.

We're kidding, of course. But what if we did do that? The book wouldn't be worth the paper it's printed on. (Or the digital bits and bytes would be just wasting space on the cloud.) And probably you would have stopped reading a long time ago. The total lack of a plan would reflect poorly on all the work we do at the National Center for Fathering. And the emptiness of our efforts would result in a disturbing echo.

So it is with our lives as fathers. We need a plan. We need to be intentional. We need to approach our role as fathers with a purpose.

So what about you? What has God called you to be and to do? Not just your career, but the very focus of your life. If you had to answer those questions today, would you have a confident answer or just make it up as you go?

The sad truth is that many dads drift through life, dealing with issues as they arise. They don't have a plan. As Andy Stanley has written, "Everybody ends up somewhere in life. A few people end up somewhere on purpose."

No wonder many dads wake up one day asking, *How did my daughter grow up so fast? Where did my son's childhood go?*

That's why it's so important to identify the unique purpose God has given each one of us. Yours is not the same as your neighbor's purpose or your accountability partner's purpose, and it's not your father's purpose. The Bible reminds us that we are each individual masterpieces and we each have our own work to do (Ephesians 2:10 NLT), so we shouldn't get bogged down comparing ourselves to others.

> Pay careful attention to your own work, for then you will get the satisfaction of a job well done, and you won't need to compare yourself to anyone else (Galatians 6:4 NLT).

So there's no use trying to live up to someone else's expectations or comparing yourself to what other guys are doing. No, your job is to concern yourself with the mission and the direction God has given you.

We could spend the next few pages listing options for you. But even if we listed a thousand goals and character traits, we might miss the ones God has for you.

Consistent Scripture study, prayer, engagement with other men and women of faith, and cultivation of your servant's heart will all go a long way toward uncovering your life's direction and purpose. As a man and as a father.

No matter how diligent we are crafting this chapter or entire book, it's really up to you to keep discovering and refining your purpose and striving to work within it. Pursue your calling with passion. Have a sense of mission. Don't just drift along and make it up as you go.

"A man without a mission is just taking up space and using up oxygen. Don't be that man."

—BROCK GRIFFIN

24

The One-Step Rule

Mike and Joey—father and son—would often shoot hoops in the driveway, and Joey really took to the sport. Many times they played semi-competitive games of HORSE—where players have to make the shot the opponent made. If they miss, they get a letter.

Early on, they agreed to the one-step rule. When Mike made a shot, Joey could go to that spot and take one step toward the basket before taking his shot. They played this way for hour after hour, year after year. As Joey got older, they did away with the rule.

But then came that inevitable day when Joey reached a certain age, a certain level of skill, and a certain teenage cockiness. He grabbed the ball and said, "Ready to play, Dad?"

"Sure—let me get my shoes on."

Joey continued, "One-step rule?"

Mike stopped and looked at his son. "You've got to be kidding! You don't need that step anymore."

Then came the punch line Joey had been waiting for years to deliver. "Not for me, Dad. I was gonna give you a step."

If you have teens or young adults, maybe you've been in Mike's high-tops. When our kids are small, we let up a little when we compete with them, maybe even letting them win once in a while. It's good for them to get a taste of victory.

A little later, when they're grade-school age kids, we have a two-part goal. First, to be a worthy competitor, helping them to hone their skills. Second, to let them know that old Dad is still king of the court and worthy of their respect.

But inevitably, there comes a time when it takes our best effort just to maintain some level of self-esteem as an athlete. They match us shot for shot on the driveway, golf course, tennis court, Ping-Pong table, and shooting range. It's even-steven.

And then one day they pass us by.

Isn't that the goal? Sure, it can be tough on the ego the first few times, but it should really be a true source of joy to see your kids grow, learn, and surpass the skill level of their old man.

The best part is that you don't even have to admit your skills and quickness are declining. Instead, take full credit for honing your amazing children into athletic superstars who are even more gifted than you are.

But don't get too far ahead of yourself. It's probably a good idea not to be spending their million-dollar signing bonus quite yet.

> *"Some of our most rewarding moments occur when our children achieve things we could never do ourselves."*
>
> **—CAREY CASEY**

25

Arrows in the Hands of a Warrior

One of the most inspiring passages of Scripture for dads is in Psalm 127.

> Children born to a young man are like arrows in a warrior's hands. How joyful is the man whose quiver is full of them! He will not be put to shame when he confronts his accusers at the city gates (Psalm 127:4-5 NLT).

We often encourage dads to read the entire psalm and meditate often on what it says to them as dads. There's a lot to chew on. And the passage applies to every season of fathering: filling your quiver, enjoying the gift, letting those arrows fly.

Author and pastor John Piper points out an aspect of this passage we probably don't often consider. Many of us think about our children and their future and dream of happiness, security, and a life free of major trials. That's natural for most dads.

But that might also be a little bit naive. This passage makes it clear our children are like arrows in a quiver. Arrows have a purpose beyond the quiver. They are shaped and sharpened for a reason. Your arrows will eventually be used in a life-and-death battle, shot with skill and precision right at the heart of the enemy.

Who is the enemy? It's the evil one, who has made disturbing progress in turning much of our culture against the ways of God. So according to this passage, we should view our children as weapons aimed carefully to penetrate the heart of a generation currently being dragged down by evil.

Ron Brown, a coach, author, and good friend of NCF, adds this: "Our children are not mantel pieces, decorations, or stuffed animals. Rather, they are called into battle."

Those are strong words, but words we must heed. So, Dad, let's make sure we equip our children for battle. Teach them biblical truth. Model a life of faith. Let them know the realities of spiritual warfare. Make sure they understand that Satan is not a cartoon character with red horns and a pitchfork. He is the deceiver, the father of lies. Train your children to bring Jesus into their daily lives, their activities, and their relationships. Reward them when they take a stand for Christ and call on his name. Point out verses of Scripture that call them to battle or claim victory in the name of Christ—such as 1 John 5:4, which promises, "Everyone born of God overcomes the world."

As parents, it's a little scary. But we have to remind ourselves that our role is one of stewardship, not ownership. Our goal is to help our children to be straight arrows and to help them identify the target God has chosen for their lives. That full quiver we carry should one day be empty.

> "As steadfast archers, we're called to sharpen and burnish our arrows, help them choose the right target, hold them close to our heart, and then— perhaps most difficult for a father—to let them fly."
>
> **—JAY PAYLEITNER**

26

How Does a Dad Look Like?

Each spring, in several states across the country, the National Center for Fathering has the privilege of helping organize Father of the Year essay contests. We invite students from kindergarten through high school to write an essay on the topic, "What My Father Means to Me."

As you can imagine, the responses cover a range of family environments, childhood wisdom, and emotions. Reviewing these thousands of essays always leads to a new appreciation of the importance of fathers. Not to mention a torrent of smiles, laughter, heartache, and tears.

We receive essays written about fathers, stepfathers, grandfathers, and father figures. Once in a while, an essay comes in from a boy or girl who has no father at all.

A second grader named Dino provided one of the more memorable entries we've ever received. His English isn't perfect, but we wanted to share his essay just as he wrote it:

> My dad passed away when I was born. I wish my dad was with my family. I wish my dad was back with me. I miss my dad a lot.
>
> I want to know how my dad looks like. Is a dad bigger than a mom? Is a dad like a grandpa? Is he big? How does a dad look like?
>
> Does he yell at you? Is he mean? Is he nice? Is a dad funny? Does he cook? Does he eat a lot? Does a dad drink beer? Does a dad play basketball?

Is a dad more special than a mom? I just want to know how my dad would be like if he were alive today. I really wish he was with me now.

What's fascinating about many of these essays is the simple, innocent way kids will put something charming right next to something heartbreaking. Dino's words capture the emptiness and the longing kids feel when their dads aren't there.

One of the real benefits of these essay contests is that the fathers usually get to read what their children have written about them. They feel honored, humbled, and challenged by those words.

But today, since Dino's father will not hear those words, we encourage you to imagine what your children would write about you. What would they say a dad looks like? Does he yell? Is he mean? Is he nice? Is a dad funny? Does a dad play basketball? Does he pray with his kids every day? Does a dad have a twinkle in his eyes?

Your children may or may not sit down to write an essay honoring you. But even today you are writing on their hearts in clear and unspoken ways. Do your kids know who you are? Or do you close yourself off from their world? Are they getting answers to their questions? Or do they live with a sense of uncertainty and helplessness?

Your unconditional love, consistent presence, and welcoming spirit will go a long way toward giving your kids the security they need to move ahead in life with confidence and courage.

"Without dads, kids can't really be kids."

—CAREY CASEY

27

Let Yourself Laugh

A dad named Richard was reading with his four-year-old son. Little Matt wanted one more book, but Richard said it was time for bed. You've been there, right?

In recent months, Richard and his wife had been helping Matt practice making wise decisions by offering choices during regular interactions. These parents typically gave Matt two perfectly reasonable options and let him choose. The strategy establishes boundaries while giving the kids a sense of personal responsibility in day-to-day matters. Not a bad idea.

Well, on this night Richard found out that Matt was catching on to their system...sort of. When Richard said again, "Sorry, son, no more books tonight," Matt came back with, "Okay, Dad, would you rather read me another book or have me poke you in the eye?"

That's a sharp kid. And that's also one of those priceless moments that makes you laugh, roll your eyes, hug your kid, and give him noogies all at the same time.

The story reminds us that if we make ourselves available, fatherhood can bring an incredible measure of joy to our lives. Too often, though, we allow the serious and sober realities of raising children to overwhelm our spontaneous and playful sides.

We need to remember that laughter promotes health—physically, developmentally, and relationally. It also helps develop higher creative and coping skills because humor and creativity both draw on divergent thinking—bringing out new and unique insight required to solve problems and respond to changing situations.

Dad, I'm sure you've experienced the power of laughter with your children. If things are tense, a good dose of laughter can open doors and restore a positive outlook. You're likely to have better communication within your family as well. Laughter makes you more approachable—especially if you can laugh at yourself.

Humor is a great strategy for connecting with children of any age, but you have to know how to get to their funny bone. Make it a point, Dad, to immerse yourself in their world so you can figure out what makes them laugh. Hang out together, read their books, and listen to their stories. If they're watching TV, plop down on the couch next to them and just enjoy their company. If you can share a funny tweet or YouTube video, that's a bonus.

It starts with playing peek-a-boo when they're babies. Before long, they're enjoying slapstick comedy and eventually quick-witted satire. So, Dad, let yourself laugh. Step out of your comfort zone and enter the unpredictable, imaginative, and often make-believe world of your children.

We're reminded once again of Psalm 127:3 (NLT), which proclaims, "Children are a gift from the LORD." They aren't burdens—they're gifts! It's up to us to be joyful, energetic, and humorous stewards of those gifts from God. In today's world, busy families can never have too much laughter and joy.

> *"Why is it that we laugh when the baby burps at the dinner table, but with a teenager, not so much?"*
>
> **—JAY PAYLEITNER**

28

A Conversation at the Drive-In

Have you thought about the young man your daughter will marry someday? She has! We know that because a dad named Mark told us about a recent conversation he had with his 11-year-old daughter during a daddy-daughter date to a drive-in movie.

As they waited for the show to start, out of the blue the preteen daughter said, "Dad, it's kinda weird to think about who you're going to marry."

Mark nearly choked on his soft drink. He never expected a statement like that from his little girl. But there she was, moving beyond schoolyard chatter and starting a conversation about something *real*.

Mark quickly regained his composure. "Hmm. What kind of husband do you think God wants for you?"

Without hesitation, she began rattling off traits she felt were important in a husband. Clearly she had been thinking about this for a while. Wisely, Mark tried to keep listening and not critique her ideas too quickly. As the list grew, Mark came to a powerful and sobering realization: She was describing *him* and how he treats her mom.

Dad, that shouldn't be a surprise. You are a key role model for your children when it comes to the many aspects of manhood, including being a husband. Your daughter especially is watching you and filing away memories of what makes—or doesn't make—a good husband.

Maintaining a great marriage is a challenge. There are daily sacrifices and obstacles, and in our most selfish moments we might not give our best effort. We might entertain Satan's lie that if it doesn't make *us* happy, it isn't worth it.

As a husband, you are called to be a servant leader and to put your bride's needs above your own. And as a dad, you're given an additional motive for being a godly and gracious mate.

Just think of your daughter ten, fifteen, or twenty years from now. Your words and actions as a husband today may very well be reflected in her marriage. She's watching you when you're thoughtful, kind, and appreciative. She's also well aware of those times when you're angry, dismissive, and demanding.

Dad, go ahead and have high expectations for your future son-in-law. Your wonderful daughter deserves a wonderful guy. No pressure, but you may want to ask yourself if you are living up to those same high expectations right now in your own marriage.

By the way, your son is also watching. He doesn't realize it, but he's making decisions right now about how he will treat his bride and his children years from now. And you're his teacher.

One more thought. Pick a nice night this week, pile the kids in the car, and find a good family movie playing at the drive-in on the edge of town.

"Our sons and daughters are watching, and they see it all."

—JAY PAYLEITNER

★ ★ ★

29

Discipline with Respect

As an involved dad, you won't be surprised by the three steps to good discipline:

- Communicate your expectations.
- When those expectations are not met, get all the facts.
- Be consistent to enforce appropriate consequences.

Those textbook answers are a good place to start. But how we carry out these steps makes all the difference.

For example, we need to ask ourselves a few questions:

- *Am I ticked off because my child dared to challenge me?*
- *Am I out to prove a point or put him back in his place?*
- *Am I reacting in the heat of the moment just because I know I need to do something?*

We are called to shape our children's behavior, but we don't have the right to belittle them in the process. We have to show them respect, even in their worst moments and no matter what they say or how they respond to us. They might disrespect us, but we cannot disrespect them.

Think about this: If one of your friends were in a bad mood, you wouldn't start yelling at him to shape up. You'd never say, "I can't believe I have to put up with this from you!" Surely our kids deserve at least that much consideration. It's sad to say, but we've seen people treat their pets with more respect than they show their children.

Going back to the three steps to discipline, respect begins with how you lay out expectations. Communicate clearly about this and have your child repeat it back to you. Make sure they understand the boundaries and consequences. Leave no room for confusion or wiggling out of it.

When your child does slip up, show empathy, not anger. Parents who yell at their kids make *themselves* the consequence. Emotions and harsh comments take center stage, and the natural consequences of your children's mistakes get lost in the process. If you lose your cool, you've also lost the chance to make this a teachable moment. The only things kids learn when dads are yelling are how to be afraid, how to be confused, and how to yell themselves.

By showing empathy and sadness instead of anger—even as we're enforcing unpleasant consequences—we can tone down the emotions and keep responsibility on their shoulders for solving the problem and addressing the character issue for next time.

Finally, by talking through the facts of the wrongdoing and the reason for the discipline, you underscore that you and the young culprit are really both on the same side. Taking that extra moment also gives you a chance to make sure you and your child's mom are on the same page and ensures that any discipline is fair, reasonable, and consistent.

Discipline isn't fun. It can be one of the great conundrums of parenting. But if you begin with a sense of empathy and respect, you're much more likely to convey the message you're trying to teach. Which means in the future you may be required to discipline less. Wouldn't that be nice?

> *"If we don't discipline our children, they will never learn to discipline themselves."*
>
> **—CAREY CASEY**

30

Raising Countercultural Kids

Cultural commentators point out that the role of parents has changed dramatically in the last couple of generations. Forty or fifty years ago, our parents or grandparents raised children to *follow the culture*. They wanted their children to learn how to conform to the messages they were hearing from the adults in their lives.

Of course, those messages were far different back then. The predominant leaders and opinion shapers were ministers, teachers, neighbors, and political leaders. Those people's words almost always agreed with our grandparents' values and worldview. Parents could focus with confidence on teaching the next generation to say yes to the dominant cultural messages around them.

Clearly, things have changed. In the '60s, the term "countercultural" meant rebellious and "if it feels good, do it." But today, we may very well *want* to raise our children to be countercultural—to say no to many of the influences around them. The dominant views of our culture are often not in line with God's Word, and we don't want our children to adopt them.

Our children hear all kinds of messages through the media, and in recent years the job of a God-fearing parent became standing in the line of fire. That meant monitoring what's on the television or computer screen, checking out movies before our kids go watch them, and educating ourselves about music artists before our kids listen.

Even though many schoolteachers exhibited solid values in the '70s,

'80s, and '90s, parents had to learn to keep up with what their children were hearing in the classroom and at required assemblies. Parents could not be sure their neighbors and the parents of their children's friends shared their values. The parenting challenge was to hold back the culture.

In the twenty-first century, because of the onslaught and availability of digital media, the role of parents has changed again. As technology advances and our children get older, we can no longer expect to protect our kids. We must assume they will be exposed to more graphic images and dangerous ideas than we can possibly intercept. The new standard of Christian parenting must be to prepare our children to be aware, be vigilant, and respond accordingly. To equip them to face the culture, recognize the negative influence, and say no.

To be clear, that doesn't let us off the hook. It's true we are no longer being a shield. Instead, we're being called to equip our kids to recognize the danger on their own and to provide them with tools and knowledge to turn away or fight back. Which means we need to be even more watchful and better informed and to engage our kids with a higher degree of love, respect, communication, and partnership.

It isn't easy, but that is the clear call for those of us who want to lead our families to know and serve God. Our mandate is to coach our children about values and truth, lead them through our modeling, and establish solid, reliable reference points in an ever-changing culture.

"The culture has lost the war—the people of God cannot."

—CAREY CASEY

★ ★ ★

31

Hope for Divorced Dads

Not long ago, we heard from a divorced dad we'll call Mike. He's been through some difficult trials and made some mistakes that became roadblocks for a relationship with his daughter.

But recently Mike's daughter contacted him and indicated she wants to be part of his life. The problem is, Mike feels paralyzed. He can't forgive himself for the sins of his past. It really seems as if his daughter authentically hopes to reconnect. She has a fathering deficit she's trying to fill. But something is holding Mike back from fully engaging with her.

Mike isn't alone. Millions of other divorced dads endure all kinds of guilt, fear, frustration, and regrets. The relationships these men have with their children are often muddled and confusing. Sometimes they're wrapped in antagonism or anger. Sometimes dads and their kids have simply come to the conclusion that it's not worth the effort and that trying to reconnect is just asking for trouble.

At NCF, we honor and root for men who want to spend time with their children. We hear from guys who might not see their children for months at a time because of work responsibilities, military duty, where the mother lives, or other factors. It's possible that time apart can bring a new perspective and sense of hope, as in the adages "Time heals all wounds" and "Absence makes the heart grow fonder." If you've been unplugged, your child may be ready for a fresh start.

On the other hand, many divorced or unmarried dads live under the assumption that their children are better off without them, or they just don't want to stir things up. There are adages that cover that perspective as well. "Out of sight, out of mind." "Let sleeping dogs lie." "Don't upset the applecart."

Our friend Mike agrees there are no easy answers and there may well be a load of painful memories and sins to overcome. Still, if you identify with this challenge, we want to offer a few simple truths.

First, your children still need you to be their dad. They know that they are part of you and always will be. They need you to be strong—strong in patience, courage, and love.

Second, there is still time. Don't be deceived into thinking there's no hope. As a divorced dad, your past may not be pretty, or maybe you've been treated unjustly by the system. Still, if the door is shut today, there's a good chance it will open tomorrow. Hope and optimism are healthy traits for any dad at any time.

Third, if your circumstances or other people are making it difficult for you to be a father, don't give up. Things do change, just as they did with Mike's daughter. Kids grow up, gain some new life experiences, realize this world is not perfect, and start putting things together. That leads to new realizations that may include a forgiving heart and a desire to know their dad in a deeper way.

In situations like Mike's—and maybe like yours—we hope, trust, pray, and believe a fresh opportunity to reconnect will come. So be ready. Your best strategy is to live with integrity today, make healthy decisions, seek God's guidance, and keep loving your kids. Even if it's from a distance. It would be a shame if you did something now that might jeopardize that opportunity when it comes.

"Be joyful in hope, patient in affliction, faithful in prayer."

—ROMANS 12:12

32

Listen to Your Daughter

Wouldn't it be nice to know exactly what your daughter wants from you? We're not talking about a pony, designer jeans, the latest Barbie or American Girl doll, or a Mazda Miata. We're talking about what she really, really wants.

We asked that question not long ago at a father-daughter event sponsored by NCF. Our goal was to help dads and their girls overcome some of the barriers that keep them from really connecting.

At one point, we asked the daughters to write an anonymous response to this statement: "Dad, I wish you would…"

We had a variety of responses. Good news—very few were materialistic requests. Actually, we were struck by one common theme that emerged in an overwhelming number of responses—*listening*. As we read and documented the words of these young women, it became clear that communication is a common challenge for dads and daughters.

There are always two sides to that problem, but since this is a book for dads, let's focus on what you can learn from what they wrote. Dad, we should warn you…you may hear your daughter's voice in these responses.

- "I wish my dad would try to understand what I'm going through and be there when I need someone to talk to just as a friend and not as a parent."

- "I need him to completely hear me out and not assume things...to listen before he speaks."

- "Take time and not talk but let me tell him one secret that I have hidden for a long time."

- "Try to see where I'm coming from before blowing up in my face and later wanting my forgiveness."

- "Listen when I need you to. You don't have to have the right answers all the time. Just be there for me."

- "I wish my dad would just listen to me and not try to make everything about him."

- "If my dad would listen and forgive me without always a punishment, I would open up and tell him more! I don't because I'm scared of getting grounded."

- "Actually stop and listen...don't think about what you're going to say, but hear and understand what I'm saying."

- "I wish he would speak calmly, not in a tone of voice that scares me."

- "Listen to me [without trying] to fix the problem or discipline me for it, but just listen."

- "Don't talk, don't argue, just listen."

There were many more, but you get the point. So, did you hear your daughter's voice? If you didn't, then you *really do* need to work on your listening skills.

> "One of the most beautiful sounds in the whole world for a father is hearing his daughter ask, 'Daddy, can we talk?'"
>
> **—JAY PAYLEITNER**

Off to College

It's exciting and yet traumatic. It's rewarding and yet heartbreaking. The year or so before a child heads off to college is a mix of emotions, memories, and planning.

On one hand, your child is pulling away from you. Whether they admit it or not, they're trying to figure out how to build a life without you. On the other hand, they're probably really scared and could use a few words of wisdom and encouragement from dear old dad.

Expect lots of ups and downs.

Every kid is different. Some are successful in high school but overwhelmed in college. Others don't do well in high school but blossom in college. You can't be sure, but it's good to take inventory of where your child is as you help them through that transition. Here are five major areas to consider.

Finances. Help your child understand how to budget their money and how some expenses are fixed, some are variable, and some are periodic. Help them think through all their possible expenses and plan wisely. Remember that they'll have to learn some money lessons by making mistakes.

Personal care. Things like laundry, hygiene, tidiness, and setting your own alarm clock. It's amazing how many college kids never learned to get themselves up and going in the morning. Dorm life can get pretty nasty pretty quickly if laundry stacks up, showers get skipped, and deodorant runs out.

Academics. Clearly, a high school graduate should be taking full responsibility for their schoolwork. On campus, they'll need proven study habits and time-management skills. And here's a clue lost on many college freshman: Go to class! And stay awake!

Social. What kinds of situations will your child be facing at college? What kinds of friends or dating relationships should they avoid? Have a lot of what-if conversations, especially about roommates, personal space, alcohol, drugs, fraternities and sororities.

Spiritual life. You can't live out their faith for them, but you can help them locate a good church and identify campus groups that will keep them plugged in. A huge percentage of students who were involved in church through high school give it up at college. Offering encouragement in this area will be much more effective than nagging and badgering. Send notes. Pray. Use calls, texts, and email to check in regularly about how your child is doing with his entire college experience and especially his faith walk.

Those are five areas you'll want to kick around and discuss for several months before freshman orientation. If you wait until the car is packed and expect to cover all of these issues while driving to registration, you'll miss out on hours of good conversations that will help them—and you—get through their freshman year.

One more suggestion. When your son or daughter takes off for that first year of college, don't immediately turn their bedroom into a sewing room, study, home gym, or office. Leave the posters up and the desk untouched. At Thanksgiving and Christmas, they're going to want to come home, flop on their old bed, and be flooded with memories of what it was like to be in a home filled with love and laughter.

"It's hard to watch your little boy or girl head off to college, but hasn't that been the goal for the last 18 years?"

—CAREY CASEY

34

Investing Time

People often use an expression that is pretty harmless in itself, but as fathers we need to think differently about it. It's the simple concept of *spending* time.

We say, "I spent a lot of time on that project," or "I spent 20 minutes standing in line at the store." Even here at NCF, we have often talked about how much time a father spends with his children. Committed fathers spend lots of time with their children, right?

Nothing is wrong with saying that, but we want to make a distinction that's worth keeping in mind as we manage our schedules and make time for our families. You see, we have to think of time as something we invest, not something we spend.

There's an obvious parallel in the financial world. If you put your money in an IRA, a mutual fund, stocks, or whatever, assuming you choose wisely, the money is still there, and its value has probably grown. It's still yours. You've chosen to use it for a specific purpose. You invested it to help you reach a particular goal.

Even when you buy other things, you feel as if you've spent your money on them, but they're still investments: a new motorcycle or big-screen TV, an exotic vacation, or even the monthly bills you pay, such as the utility bill or your rent or mortgage payment. They are all investments you choose to make. Some bring valuable long-term dividends. Some are more like tossing a fistful of cash into the wind.

Wise stewards invest in things that last and bring a high rate of return. They leverage their resources to bring about the most benefits. And of course, the funds are always limited. So if you're investing money in one place, you've chosen *not* to invest it in another place. When it's gone, it's gone!

We hope you're catching the analogy. Your time is a commodity—perhaps your most valuable commodity. Every minute you spend with your kids is an investment in your relationship with them. Of course, that includes the ski trip to Aspen and weekends at Disney. But perhaps even more valuable are the times you take your seven-year-old with you to the hardware store or join the stuffed animals at a tea party with your little girl. Don't forget dinner table conversations, campfire stories, tucking in, and just lying in the grass looking for cloud shapes and talking about hopes and dreams. Those are all high-yield investments.

Because time is also a limited resource, you'll need to budget and prioritize. If you're the family breadwinner, much of your time will go toward providing financially for your family, and that's a noble and worthy cause. But if that investment takes you away from family events and activities, you're creating a deficit that's piling up like debt, and you may be headed for disaster at home.

So keep investing those minutes, days, and hours. On a regular basis, ask yourself and ask your bride if it's time to make some changes in your time portfolio.

> "A time to be born and a time to die, a time to plant and a time to uproot, a time to kill and a time to heal, a time to tear down and a time to build, a time to weep and a time to laugh, a time to mourn and a time to dance..."
>
> **—ECCLESIASTES 3:2-4**

35

Five A.M. Basketball

James is a busy man with many professional and community responsibilities. He's also a devoted father. Several years ago, James's son developed a burning passion for the game of basketball—and he had some skills.

Watching his son, James saw a spark. Some real potential. Now, we know that sometimes dads go a little crazy pushing their kids and try to live vicariously through them. But involved dads are also most likely to see a child's gifts and recognize the need for a nudge or a challenge to take it up a notch. And that's what James did.

One day, James suggested his son go beyond just attending practice. He presented the idea of putting in a little more effort than his teammates and seeing where that might lead. James had seen the boy's passion and simply explained that if he really wanted to excel, it was going to take more time, more commitment.

As he challenged his son, James realized that in order to really make it stick, he needed to demonstrate that same commitment himself. So he agreed to go to the gym with his boy every day at five a.m., which meant getting up at four something. That's a pretty significant commitment.

At first it was just the two of them. They'd play one-on-one, shoot, and run drills. After a while, some of the son's friends heard about this and started coming as well, and occasionally other fathers came too. But James was consistent. He was there every day for his son. You can imagine the positive impact this had on their relationship.

Here's the rest of the story. The son earned a scholarship and went on to play college basketball. As a freshman, he was the starting shooting guard and led the conference in three-point percentage. Of course, James attends just about every game even though the college is out of state, requiring lots of extra travel.

At NCF, we applaud this kind of fathering. We also like to think that what James did is within the reach of all dads. He simply saw a chance to partner with his son and took the next step. That's what dads do. Today, James would confirm that even if his son never went on to play college ball, the sacrifice was well worth the reward. Believe it or not, he even misses those five a.m. workouts.

We especially like this story because it touches on all five fundamentals of Championship Fathering (one of the hallmarks of the National Center for Fathering): loving, coaching, modeling, encouraging other kids, and enlisting other dads.

Those five ideals are the foundation of all we do at NCF and are woven throughout the pages of this book. Carey even wrote a book titled *Championship Fathering*. Also, the fathers.com website provides a link where you can download a Championship Fathering commitment card and be part of the effort to change the culture for today's children and generations to come.

> "With Championship Fathering, we're seeking to reach, teach, and unleash a multitude of committed dads, creating a national movement that can strengthen families and reverse the negative trends of fatherlessness in our society."
>
> **—CAREY CASEY**

36

Can I Call You "Daddy" Too?

This book wouldn't be complete if we didn't include at least one giant plug for fathers to volunteer to be WatchDOGS (Dads of Great Students).

You already know that the National Center for Fathering has all kinds strategies and plans to connect dads and kids. But WATCH D.O.G.S. may be the most surprising, fun, and rewarding of all our programs. Simply explained, it's an organized way for dads to spend a day volunteering in their children's school.

A couple of stories will make clear the value of the program.

During his day as a WatchDOG, Eric was surprised to see how many kids at the school wanted to get close to him. As he escorted the kindergartners to their activities, different kids walked next to him and grabbed his hand. Several seemed especially hungry for his attention.

A few kids even opened up and told him, "I don't have a dad," or "My dad doesn't live with me anymore." One girl, a friend of Eric's daughter, cried as she told him how hurt she was that her father had left. Eric says, "It broke my heart. I never realized how much this simple day as a volunteer could affect me on an emotional level."

On the way home, Eric asked his daughter what she thought about his day at her school, and she said at first it was hard. But since some kids don't have fathers, it felt good to share him with her friends for a day.

A similar story comes from a man named Chuck who also spent a day as a WatchDOG dad. As he helped out in his son's class, a young boy latched onto him. The boy kept hearing Chuck's son call him "Daddy" and asked him if that was his name. Apparently, he didn't even know what the word "daddy" meant. Chuck explained what a daddy is, and then the boy asked if he could call Chuck "Daddy" also. Chuck put his arm around the boy's shoulders and said, "Yeah, that would be fine." Chuck told us, "It broke my heart." Then he added this: "I'd like to think that in some tiny way I helped that young man feel accepted and loved. Most of us never have to question whether our fathers love us or whether our kids know they are loved, but moments like that remind you just how great a blessing a father's love truly is."

If you have school-age kids, you may want to consider introducing WATCH D.O.G.S. in your community. NCF has staff dedicated to making that easy for you and your child's school.

But regardless of whether you participate in the WATCH D.O.G.S. program, you have plenty of opportunities to invest in the lives of kids who need what a father provides. All you have to do is look around. As these stories show, it doesn't take that much—just a word of encouragement, a listening ear, an arm around the shoulder.

Eric and Chuck will never forget the kids they met that day. Will you also be intentional about reaching out and encouraging kids in need?

> *"Every dad should be a WatchDOG once or twice a year."*
>
> **—CAREY CASEY**

★ ★ ★

37

Be a Dad Today, Not Someday

Dad, have you put off a family vacation because of money? Or maybe you decided not to have or adopt another child because you couldn't afford it. Maybe your kids had to quit Tae Kwon Do or gymnastics because bills were piling up.

We understand those decisions, and we need to be responsible stewards of what God has entrusted to us. But as we lead our families, we should also make the most of the moments we have—even if they cost some money. We are also stewards of the opportunities God brings our way.

It's like our friend Todd Wilson at familymanweb.com says: Despite the turbulent stock market, the slumping housing market, rising energy costs, and the uneasiness of the global economy, there has never been a better time to be a dad.

Now, we're not suggesting you go hog wild on extravagant gifts and trips. Sticking to a budget, minimizing debt, and setting long-range goals are noble habits that provide worthy lessons for our children. But if we're talking about denying your family a meaningful time now so you can pump more dollars into your retirement fund—well, that's something you really need to pray about.

Financial advisor Larry Burkett used to say, "Don't sacrifice the present to save for a future that may never come."

This next summer is your only chance to go camping with your kids *at this age*. Now might be the best window of opportunity for them to develop skills in music, sports, or art. Your son only turns 13 once—don't let money keep you from getting away for a few days and having those important talks.

It doesn't make sense to pack away thousands of dollars for the proverbial "someday" and then say you can't afford a regular date night with your wife or an occasional anniversary trip.

So, Dad, make those reservations for that family trip. Say yes to those sports lessons at the local rec club. Your son or daughter doesn't have to have the most expensive baseball glove, lacrosse stick, or cleats on the team. But they need to have gear that helps make them better, not worse.

If your child shows an aptitude for filmmaking, photography, ballet, gymnastics, figure skating, music, architecture, web design, or some other endeavor that takes a financial investment, prepare to stretch yourself. Don't mortgage the house. But also don't have regrets that you didn't support their dreams.

When you think about it, it's actually a privilege to help children identify and nurture their talents. You certainly can't put a price on making memories and once in a while receiving a sincere "Thanks, Dad."

Saving money is a good thing. But don't be the guy who ends up with a huge bank account and no one to share it with. Invest in your marriage and relationships with your kids today. Because "someday" may never get here.

"Your most important day as a dad is today."

—BROCK GRIFFIN

38

Pizza Buffet

Bruce was treating his three kids and himself to an all-you-can-eat pizza buffet. From the outside, they couldn't miss the buffet price painted in huge numbers and bright colors on the window. It also advertised a cheaper price for kids age four through nine.

Since Bruce's oldest child, Parker, had just celebrated his tenth birthday, the boy took special notice of the sign and commented on it as they stood in line to pay. He was almost proud that he'd be charged the full price for his pizza. Bruce, of course, wasn't so thrilled, but with three growing kids, he had already reconciled himself to a rising food budget.

When they reached the cashier, Bruce might have been thinking about something else, or maybe he had a lapse in judgment. The cashier didn't ask how old Parker was, and she quickly rang up one adult and three children. Bruce paid the money, and they were herded through.

Wouldn't you know it—Parker is one of those kids who notices everything. So when they sat down with their plates full of "gourmet" pepperoni pie, he pointed it out. "Dad, they didn't charge us enough, did they?"

Suddenly it was very clear to Bruce that he should have paid more attention to that transaction—because it's the right thing to do and because his son was watching to see how he handled it.

"You're right, son," he said, and immediately he went back and paid the difference.

The girl at the register tried to wave him off, saying it didn't matter—it was only a dollar and a few pennies. But to Bruce, it did matter. His integrity was on the line—at least in the eyes of his children. He did the right thing eventually, but he knows he should have done it right the first time.

It wasn't a dramatic situation, but it does demonstrate the importance of modeling for our kids—a key fundamental of Championship Fathering. They're always watching us, wondering, *What's Dad going to do? How's he going to handle this one? Does he really walk the talk?*

Dad, believe me, your children will be powerfully influenced by memories of you relaxing your standards and compromising godly values, as well as the times when you went out of your way to do the right thing.

It's worth a little money—no, it's worth a lot of money—to defend your integrity and be a positive model.

> *"Having children makes you a better man. Or at least it should."*
>
> **—BROCK GRIFFIN**

39

Fathering Under a Microscope

Every day here at the National Center for Fathering, we write, speak, or think about helping guys to be better dads. It's our job. And it has undeniable fringe benefits you won't find at most other jobs.

Specifically, it makes us better dads. Without a doubt, the Casey, Griffin, and Payleitner kids have all benefited directly from insights, discoveries, and strategies their dads uncovered while we were punched in at work.

Examples are easy to come up with. When you write a blog post on the benefits of hugging, you can't help but hug your own kids the next time you see them. After you see a report on the negative impact of pornography, you become even more cautious before clicking on a website or sidebar link. After praying with a dad going through a tough season, you feel compelled to add a prayer for your own family.

We love what we do. And we promise never to take it for granted.

Still, there's sort of a downside. When we go to events at school, at church, or in our neighborhood and community, we know that quite a few people are aware of what we do for a living. Which means that how we interact with our kids and even how they turn out is being scrutinized a little more than usual. It feels as if we're held to a higher standard. We can't raise our voices in public. Our kids need to be extra polite. Their shoes need to be polished and their blue jeans creased. It would be scandalous if a child of someone who works at NCF revealed a tattoo, wore a bikini, picked their nose, or fell asleep during a Sunday service. And if the name Casey, Griffin, or Payleitner ended up in the newspaper as part of a police report, we would have to disown that child, right?

We hope you realize we're exaggerating just bit. Those concerns are probably all in our heads.

For sure, we want to be good parents. We want our kids to make good decisions. We want them to be respectful, healthy, honest, and reasonably good mannered. We want to be good role models for other dads, and we want our kids to be positive influences on their peers. That's all true for us. And it's true for you, right?

Still, let's all agree right now that no matter what we do for a living, we should not get too wrapped up in what the world might think. Here are some questions to ask ourselves in this regard:

Am I really doing what's best for my kids? Or am I motivated more by what people might think?

Do I make parenting decisions based on what the world says? Or what God says?

Do I base my love and appreciation for my children on their accomplishments? Or do I love them unconditionally?

The authors of this book confess that we don't always get it right. Because of our jobs, we may even sometimes try a little too hard to look as if we have our act together. We hope that confession doesn't cause you to slam this book in disgust. Really, it should be an encouraging concept. This should be a freeing thought. *Carey, Brock, and Jay are not perfect dads, so maybe I shouldn't beat myself up quite so much for falling short.*

So how should any God-fearing dad respond to all this? It's true that any father who calls himself a Christian has a responsibility to do his best to reflect God's love and character. The fruit of the Spirit— love, joy, peace, patience, kindness, goodness, faithfulness, gentleness, and self-control (Galatians 5:22-23)—should be woven into your own character. Even under trying circumstances, your life should reflect the knowledge and big-picture view that God is in control. That may sound like a daunting task, but really that attitude is a worthy and reachable goal. Your joy as a father and follower of Christ should be visible. Other dads may be watching our families and deciding whether to take a closer look at Jesus, open their Bibles, or get out of bed on Sunday morning to go to church.

In other words, even if you don't work at NCF, you are a role model for other men in your circle of influence. But rather than trying to be a super dad, our suggestion would be to live a life of vulnerability and humility. Show up. Do your best. And when you mess up, seek forgiveness. That's much more attractive than having perfect kids with perfect teeth and perfect SAT scores.

Our kids are going to make mistakes. And so will every father reading these words. But as long as we're living under God's grace and motivated by what's best for our children, we'll be okay—even under a microscope.

> *"Stop judging by mere appearances,*
> *but instead judge correctly."*
>
> **—JOHN 7:24**

★　★　★

40

Cracking Your Code

Travis was headed to the grocery store with two of his children tagging along. His six-year-old, Alex, asked him, "Dad, how come you always go to two different stores to buy food?"

"I don't know," Travis answered.

There was a bit of a pause, and then Alex said, "Katie says that when you say, 'I don't know,' it means you're not really listening."

In the same monotone, Travis replied, "Huh? Oh, yeah...really?"

As it turns out, Travis gave his kids plenty more lackluster, noncommittal answers during that shopping trip.

It wasn't until later that night he realized what had happened, and it stunned him. His kids had cracked his code! He had grown accustomed to giving his son and daughter instant and easy nonanswers that actually meant he wasn't listening or didn't want to make the effort to think about an answer. The stunning truth was that Travis relied on the code quite a bit, and his kids knew all about it!

We all know that sometimes a six-year-old—or a sixteen-year-old for that matter—will go on and on about something that doesn't really matter. It's just chatter; sometimes it's nonsense. But you should also know that how we listen conveys much to our children. Caring about what they're telling us demonstrates that we care for *them*.

So let's take a moment to do some quick self-diagnosis.

- Are you available to your kids? Do you want to be? How would your kids answer these questions?

- When you're alone with them—in the car, at bedtime, whenever—do they ask questions? Or have they given up because you're not listening anyway?

- Do they come to you with their child-size problems? Or have they stopped because they know you're too distracted to help?

- Finally, later on, when they have some real challenges in life, will they come to you for wisdom and advice? Or will they simply choose to make those decisions on their own?

Whatever age your kids are, listening is a skill you need to master right now. We challenge you to focus on every word from every family member for the next week. Look them in the eyes, pay attention to nonverbal cues, and really listen to what they're saying and their tone of voice. And of course, when necessary, give a thoughtful answer.

Maybe even make a game of it. When a question comes up, engage them in conversation and keep talking until they learn something from you and you learn something from them.

Have your kids cracked your codes? They're pretty smart, so don't be surprised if they have. Besides, that means they're listening to you. And isn't that what family members do?

> *"When you listen to your children, you're telling them, 'You matter to me, you matter to the world, and you matter to God.'"*
>
> **—CAREY CASEY**

41

Being Unfaithful as a Father

There seems to be a double standard when it comes to the personal lives of leaders in America.

When a highly visible person in the world of business, politics, education, or religion is discovered to have significant moral failures, there is outrage—and there should be. That person is held accountable. Stockholders, voters, congregation members, or the public demand change. Even if the leader is not ousted or suspended, at least the public agrees that mistakes were made.

But when leaders are "unfaithful" as fathers, people barely notice. There's not even a ripple. It's become routine and acceptable for men to neglect their children so they can pursue so-called "success" at their jobs. Such men are even applauded and honored as committed leaders.

Fortune magazine recently quoted one CEO who told his company, "I don't see my family much. My family is you." Another high-profile CEO who has an 18-year-old daughter reported working 100-hour weeks for the past 20 years.

Penelope Trunk, a news columnist in Virginia, wrote, "If you are poor and you abandon your kids you are a bad parent. But if you are rich and you abandon them to run a company, you're profiled in *Fortune* magazine."[1]

Dads, we know how it is. Your career can gradually drag you away from your family. It's a lot like the way some men are lured into being unfaithful to their wives. It's never one intentional bad choice. It's taking your eyes off what's really important and focusing on some goal that can never be as satisfying as you might think. Suddenly you look up and you've lost your way.

Work will always present you with tough choices. Sure, you have to provide for your family, and that can be a noble and rewarding quest. But work can also tempt you with wealth, power, and prestige. It's a mistress that can easily dislodge you from your family and hamper communication with your children.

In Ecclesiastes 1:14, Solomon tells, "I have seen all the things that are done under the sun; all of them are meaningless, a chasing after the wind." Sadly, some dads reach retirement age, look back on their lives, and realize they spent too much time chasing after the wind and not enough time pursuing relationships with those they love—especially their children.

Make sure you're not that guy. Today and every day, ask God to give you fresh eyes to see how you're spending your time and whether you're investing enough of yourself in the lives of your children.

We've found a simple yet challenging way to guard against a gradual shifting of your priorities. We recommend a regular assessment of how you're navigating work and family responsibilities. But it's not just a checklist you track on your own. The challenge is that you need to find the courage to be accountable to your wife and older children.

Ask them, "Am I out of balance?" "Are you getting the leftovers of my time and attention?" "Does my job serve our family, or is it the other way around?"

If you're a CEO, shift supervisor, head coach, senior pastor, executive director, account manager, or leader in some other role, this may be a humbling experience. But you have to admit, the answers to those kinds of questions are exactly what you need to know.

So ask your family. Then really listen. And take their comments to heart.

"Men often fool themselves into thinking they are irreplaceable at work, when actually it's within their family they can never be replaced."

—BROCK GRIFFIN

★　★　★

42

Bond with Your Baby

When a new baby comes into the world, we dads don't always get the support and encouragement we need to make a smooth transition into fatherhood. Relating to our little bundle of joy can be intimidating. This is new territory we're exploring. And our wives suddenly have a whole new set of priorities. No wonder some dads are hesitant, they feel a disconnect with their newborn, and they're frightened of making a mistake.

Well, Daddy, take a breath. Understand that you're not the first man to be the father of a newborn. And be sure of this: Your child needs you to be involved. Besides, we want you to soak in all the joy that comes with being a new dad. So here are five quick suggestions for bonding with your baby:

Get to know your child—and let them get familiar and comfortable with you. Meeting their physical needs is a great way to do that. Get close and talk in gentle tones. Snuggle that little one often and make a lot of eye contact. Lay on the couch and let your baby sleep on your chest. You'll be glad to discover that changing a newborn's diapers really doesn't stink very much and there's no reason for you not to master that task.

Spend some time alone with your baby. It's good for Mom to get away and have some time to herself, and she needs to learn she can trust you with the baby. The baby also needs to learn that you're dependable and they can rely on you to meet their needs. Plus, Dad, being alone with your baby gives you plenty of time to practice basic care and feeding, deal with colic, and all that good stuff.

Be willing to ask for help. You don't know everything, and you'll make mistakes. So ask the baby's mom how to do things. Tell her you know she's good at this stuff, but you want to learn it too. Talk together about joys and concerns you have from day to day.

Talk with other dads. The baby is brand-new to you, but many of your friends have been through similar experiences. Ask how they handled things and any secrets they stumbled on that made a difference.

One step at a time. We know fatherhood can seem overwhelming. Looking at your new baby, your imagination might fast-forward to reveal images of a 17-year-old getting ready for prom, a high school athlete earning a Division 1 scholarship, or a young adult receiving a standing ovation at Carnegie Hall. Don't worry or put too much pressure on yourself or that infant. There's plenty of time to get your brain wrapped around those dreams. For now, just think about what your baby needs from you today, tomorrow, and maybe a few months down the road.

> *"Dad, if you're committed to be there and meet your baby's needs, you'll do fine."*
>
> **—CAREY CASEY**

★ ★ ★

43

Heavenly Fathering

What should be our number one objective as fathers? If you filled a room with well-intentioned dads, that question might generate some good discussion. Dig through our research at NCF, and you might even be able to justify any number of answers.

Actually, the answer to the question is fairly obvious. But the objective is impossible to achieve.

The number one goal for any dad is to *model for our children what God is like as a heavenly Father.*

Again, that's impossible. God is perfect. We're not. The difference between even the best father in the world and God is, well, infinite.

Still, we have to realize and remember that many of our children's ideas about God will be based on their relationships with us. That's something we need to keep top of mind. God identified himself as a heavenly *Father.*

If a child grows up with an earthly father who is absent or emotionally distant, it will be much more difficult for them to view God as a present, actively involved heavenly Father. If a dad is inconsistent or overly harsh and rigid, his children are more likely to be tentative and fearful as they approach God.

Similarly, if you demonstrate unconditional love to your children, help them discover their gifts and talents, and empower them with sincere encouragement, they will trust their heavenly Father for those same character traits.

This is not a magic formula, but it is a guiding principle.

We always say with modeling, your kids are watching. You are already a model whether you want to be or not. But you can choose to be a good one or a bad one. Our fathering *will* create impressions about God for our children, and it's up to us to make the most of our opportunity.

How can we show them what God is like? Consider the attributes of God: He is love. He is just. He is merciful. He is slow to anger. He is available. God protects and provides. Does that sound like the kind of father you want to be? No doubt, that's the kind of father your kids need.

Dad, we know you're never going to be all-powerful, all-knowing, or always present. But if you have little ones at home, that's pretty much how they're going to see you for a while. Trust us, it won't last forever. Teenagers know very well their dad isn't perfect. Still, there should be some residual respect and trust left from their younger days.

Make every effort to reflect the character of God in your life. Which means you should probably get to know him as much as possible yourself.

> "See what great love the Father has lavished
> on us, that we should be called children
> of God! And that is what we are!"
>
> **—1 JOHN 3:1**

44

Marking Milestones

D ad, when do babies typically first crawl? Or stand? Or talk? If you're not sure, please don't feel bad. You're not alone.

A study at the University of Rochester discovered that about one-third of parents of nine-month-olds have a surprisingly low knowledge about child development milestones, such as when babies talk, learn right from wrong, or can be potty trained.[2]

Some moms and dads have unrealistic expectations for their children and become frustrated. Others underestimate their kids' abilities and prevent them from learning on their own.

Nearly all of the parents surveyed were moms, and based on our experiences and research, it's reasonable to assume that a significantly higher percentage of fathers are uninformed about their children's development—probably half to two-thirds. In many cases, dads really don't know what to expect or when to expect it. They just wing it.

The researchers also concluded that low-level knowledge of child development predicted two things in the parents. First, they are less likely to enjoy healthy interactions with their infants during learning tasks. Second, they are less likely to engage their children in regular enrichment activities.

Whether you're a new dad or your children are older, this idea of marking milestones is a big deal. Not because it's a race, but because being aware of what your child is accomplishing helps you feed into their unique interests, needs, dreams, and challenges. This insight is a big part of coaching your kids, which is one of the five fundamentals of fathering that we talk about at NCF. Coaching is the lifelong process of shaping, mentoring, and empowering a child as he or she moves toward adulthood.

Applying the researchers' conclusions about milestones makes a difference in our approach to being a dad. It can make us more motivated to engage our children in learning activities. Guys like to keep score. And if we really engage our newborns, babies, and toddlers, we'll see that they are learning something new or mastering a new skill just about every day. Lifting their heads. Turning over. Sucking their toes. Clapping their hands. Waving. Scooting. And hopefully saying their very first word, "Daddy." (Don't count on it, Dad.)

Marking milestones brings a new confidence to our fathering. When we are aware of our children's "new tricks," we can be confident our actions are making a difference—building them up, encouraging them, helping them overcome difficulties, and so on.

Whether your children are toddlers or adults, continue being aware of their unique gifts and milestones. You'll always be ready with a word of sincere encouragement. Things like, "I remember quizzing you on your multiplication tables, and now you're in advanced trigonometry." "I remember you tripping over the cracks in the sidewalk. Now you're running high hurdles." "I remember you were the last one to use full sentences at preschool. Now you're speaking at graduation."

Track all their milestones, Dad. You'll be able to see how far you and your kids have come.

> *"We can get so caught up in our own calendars and deadlines that we miss the milestone moments in the lives our children."*
>
> **—CAREY CASEY**

45

Invisible Stepdads

Let's dedicate this short chapter to stepdads. Especially the ones who feel invisible. We have a sneaking suspicion that label might apply to a few other dads as well.

Wayne wrote to us with a question common for men in his situation. He deeply cares for his stepchildren, but nearly all of his interactions with the kids come when his wife is around. The kids are older, and when his wife has to be out of town, they pretty much don't give him the time of day. They don't tell him where they're going. If they acknowledge one of his questions, they give a one-word answer. If they need help, they won't ask.

Like many stepdads, Wayne feels invisible and left out. Of course, this situation becomes a cycle, a self-fulfilling problem. As this family spends less time together, they feel less commitment and connection. Dad stops reaching out, and the stepkids have one more reason to give up on their new dad.

One author on family issues we really appreciate is Dr. Bob Barnes. When it comes to being a stepparent, he emphasizes one word over and over again: "patience."

That's not easy to hear. We want things to feel "normal," whatever that means. We want a chance to build bridges, but first we have to wait for some of the walls to fall down. As a stepdad, you've married into this family and you want things to progress. You see the potential to build a stable and happy family, and you can get frustrated when things move slowly.

But remember what has happened in the past for those kids. Going through a divorce or the death of one of their parents and then a remarriage—that isn't easy. There's a lot to figure out and adjust to. So we can't rush things.

Actually, Dr. Barnes suggests that we think in terms of how old the child was when you became his or her stepfather. That number is an indicator of how much *more* time it will probably take for you to form a strong relationship with him. That may not seem encouraging, but it may help you set realistic expectations.

So be patient, Dad. Show patience of heroic proportions. If you're expecting things to be great in a year or two, you'll be disappointed almost continually.

Discipline is a related concern here. In most cases, it's best to let the biological parent handle discipline issues. If you step in too quickly, you could very well set yourself back a few notches and a few years. If you're a stepdad in the middle of frustrating discipline issues right now, it may even be wise to talk with your bride and then have a family meeting to announce that for the next several months you're going to step back from doling out punishments. They'll breathe a sigh of relief, and you will too.

If after several years you still haven't connected with your stepchildren, we want you to know that we often hear about young men and women in their late teens and early twenties thanking their stepfathers for stepping up. And even apologizing for giving them such a hard time.

Remember, the word is "patience." Your patient attitude will validate the child's right to process things on his timetable, and it will take some of the pressure off of you as a stepdad.

> *"One of the most important and rewarding jobs in the world is being a father to a kid who didn't have one."*
>
> **—CAREY CASEY**

46

Wireless Connections

A generation ago, when a boy wanted to call a girl and ask her out on a date, the available technology created some automatic checks and balances.

First, the family phone was probably located in a central part of the house. So the boy's entire family knew who he was calling and why. They probably could hear most of what he was saying.

On the other end of the line, the girl's dad or mom likely answered the phone, and the boy had to ask to speak to her. They knew who was talking to their daughter, and they probably heard her side of the conversation. There was a natural accountability there, so both the boy and girl were on their best behavior.

But today? Well, if your son wants to call a girl, he's up in his room, using his cell phone to call her cell phone. Or maybe they're texting each other or chatting online.

That all happens without the parents even knowing they are communicating, much less whom they're talking to or what they're saying. Any accountability is gone, and if no one knows what they're doing, they're much more likely to push the boundaries of what is proper and right.

This is just one example of how technology has transformed the world in which our kids are growing up. For generations, fathers had the advantage of having more resources and wisdom at their disposal. Today, the kids seem to be a step ahead, especially when it comes to technology.

Does this mean we should deny our children smartphones and other new technologies? Probably not. Instead, we need to double our efforts to keep the lines of communication flowing. Before you sign up for a new wireless plan, talk with your kids about what they think they need and what they really need. This is your chance to talk about choices—financial, moral, relational, legal—and all the safety issues surrounding texting, sharing information, cyberbullying, and cybercrime.

Remember also that you have the right and responsibility to use that new technology to your advantage. If your teens have cell phones, they have no reason not to check in at assigned times. If they like to go out weekend nights, consider installing a locator app or some other parental control on your family's phones. It's not that you don't trust your kids, Dad. It's your job to protect them, right? Just as when they were little, we need to be aware of what our children are doing. Some might call that intrusive or overly controlling. Others might call it being a dad in an ever-changing world.

Regardless of what you decide about phones and wireless technology, the goal has been the same for generations. Work toward building strong relationships and talking openly about what's going on in your kids' lives. You need to be able to ask your son what he's been up to and know that he'll tell you the truth. Your daughter needs to trust you and know that you want what's best for her, so she has no reason not to tell you the truth.

That might sound like an unrealistic ideal, but we believe it's possible. As the world changes, we need to stay connected to our children and help guide them through the memorable and important decisions of life.

> "We can't know everything our kids do, every place our kids go, and everyone our kids hang out with, and that's probably a good thing. We have to learn to trust them, and they have to learn to trust themselves."
>
> **—JAY PAYLEITNER**

★　　★　　★

47

Parents on Different Pages

Jerry is a divorced dad. He's with his 13-year-old daughter one night a week and every other weekend. His issue is that he and his daughter's mother are setting different standards for their daughter's behavior—the clothes she wears, the grades she earns, and so on.

It's hard enough to be on the same page with your child's mother when you live together. Nearly all dads and moms have different approaches when addressing their children's behavior. One is often more strict and the other more relaxed.

When you add in different households and all the emotions of a broken relationship, it's really tough. As a dad, you might give your child a consequence for something, but then her mom doesn't back you up and enforce it. Without a doubt, the kids pick up on that and use it against you.

A friend and former staffer at NCF has been through this, and we really appreciate his insights in this regard. As the saying goes, rules without relationship lead to rebellion. As a partial-custody father, the "rules" side of the equation can be a big frustration. But how about the "relationship" side? In most cases, it's even more important to go the extra mile, making sure your children know how much you love them, value them for who they are, and are committed to their well-being.

Now, don't go overboard trying to buy their love. Kids see right through that. What they really want is your time, your respect, some sincere interaction, a dash of humility, and a dose of humor. Honesty, forgiveness, and appreciation are also important parts of the formula. As your relationship strengthens, your rules won't feel quite so oppressive. In the end, your love for your kids opens the door for effective discipline. Especially as they get older, children respond more to the relationship than the rules.

So here's the takeaway if your situation is like Jerry's. Put your relationship with your young teenage daughter first and the rules second. Then, when you object to the next fashion trend that comes along, she'll know you aren't being arbitrary or just trying to win a battle. She'll know without a doubt that you love her and really do have what's best for her in mind.

What's more, she'll respect you for taking a stand and helping her think things through. So often children who have gone through divorce are looking for more structure and security, not less. They may not say it, but they do appreciate a dad (or a stepdad) who makes reasonable, loving, and thoughtful choices on their behalf. Even if they initially disagree.

Before you know it, when your teenagers have a question about something important, they'll come to you first. They'll know and trust that every decision you make grows out of your sincere and undeniable love.

> *"When moms and dads who share custody don't get on the same page, nobody wins. Especially the kids."*
>
> **—CAREY CASEY**

48

It's Not My Job

One summer evening, Ted and Maureen were at a backyard barbecue watching their young daughter Jessie play with the other neighborhood kids. At one point, Jessie grabbed a toy away from another little girl, who began to cry.

Just about every adult within earshot was aware of the interaction. But it's not an unusual thing for toddlers to do, so no one was making any kind of judgment. But Maureen was embarrassed. "Ted," she said, "did you see what your daughter did?"

This young mom obviously expected her husband to handle the situation in a certain way. But Ted just sat there with a look that said, "Yeah...so?"

That day, Ted discovered something new and unpredicted. His wife had expectations for him as a father that he didn't even know about.

Maybe that's happened to you. It's probably more common for new dads who are trying to figure out their new role, but it's something we all need to consider. The best way to deal with expectations like this is to bring them out in the open—verbalize them—so you and your bride can discuss them and make decisions about them.

Now, don't have that discussion in front of the neighbors, but do have it. That discussion may even open the door to the bigger issue of accountability. Think about it this way: When you verbalize your commitment to follow through on certain expectations as a father, you're suddenly obliged to make it happen. You're accountable to that commitment. But if you never say what you intend to do, you can't be in the doghouse for not doing it. Please don't tell us that's your plan!

What's more, when you accept future responsibility as part of your routine expectations, you negate future opportunities to be a hero. When some dads change a diaper or intercede in a backyard toy battle, they act as if they deserve an award for making sacrifices above and beyond the call of duty. After all, anything looks great when you've committed yourself to nothing.

Expectations for fathers are often cloudy because for generations, moms typically spent much more time with the children. Dads were seen as disciplinarians or playmates. Men interacted with children only when the kids needed correction or the dads wanted to blow off some steam. Moms were taken for granted, and dads were sometimes nowhere to be found.

That attitude doesn't work anymore. When it comes to parenting, fathers are no longer an afterthought. That's good news, but the new paradigm requires dads and moms to talk through expectations and agree on the division of duties. Maybe you're in charge of bath night, supervising Saturday chores, and tucking-in duties. Mom does breakfast, arranges for childcare, and keeps the weekly calendar of playdates and carpools. Everything else on the parenting to-do list depends on who's available and requires ongoing communication.

The goal is to make sure that everything that needs doing gets done. And to create some kind of equity with your bride. And most importantly, to make sure little Jessie is loved, instructed, disciplined, and taught to share her toys. Right?

> *"It's a good thing that dads can no longer sit in a La-Z-Boy recliner with their pipe and slippers and hide behind the evening newspaper."*
>
> **—JAY PAYLEITNER**

49

New Dad, New Husband

Are you a new father? Here's an awkwardly accurate thought. In many ways, when that new baby comes, you're also getting a new wife, and you need to adjust accordingly.

For sure, you are losing out on some sleep, figuring out your new role, and learning how to bond with the little bundle of joy. Well, how about considering just for a minute what your wife is going through? She's already endured a series of transformations you couldn't begin to imagine. The physical changes of pregnancy and childbirth, the hormonal shifts and postpartum issues...In addition, think of all the challenges you're dealing with. She's experiencing *all* of them, only probably to a greater degree—the lack of sleep, bonding, figuring out where the parenting books and the advice from well-meaning aunts are wrong, and learning how to trust her instincts. Plus, nourishment for the little one is probably 90 percent her responsibility. If she's breast-feeding, that percentage goes up to nearly 100.

Along with that, she undergoes a wave of guilt whenever the baby sniffles, can't sleep, sleeps too much, or cries for no apparent reason. She thinks, *Did I eat healthy enough during my pregnancy? Was I wrong to take that cough syrup or aspirin during the first trimester? Is the baby getting enough nutrition from my breast milk?*

Conversely, when the baby is a few weeks old, you'll be going about your day and suddenly remember, *Oh, hey—I'm a new father. I had forgotten that for a minute.*

So keep reading this book and seek out other reasonable advice on being a great dad. But please realize you'll be ahead of the curve if you step it up and rededicate yourself to being a great *husband*.

First, accept that children will change your marriage. There's still plenty of love to go around. But time and attention may be in short supply. So prepare yourself to make some sacrifices. One of those areas will be in regards to romance. Hopefully that doesn't come as a shock. There will be other areas of adjustments as well. Without listing them here, let's just say, when you have conflicts and frustrations, lead your family with a generous and humble spirit.

By the way, while you're adjusting, your wife is also adjusting.

So commit to your marriage. Commit to your family. Be a servant leader. Assist your wife. Listen to her. Do the grocery shopping. Give her back rubs and foot rubs. Make late-night runs to satisfy any cravings, just as you've been doing for the previous nine months.

Be more intentional about spending time together. Once your newborn settles into a schedule, you may even be able to sneak away for a regular date night. But don't overlook the bonding that can happen between new parents just walking around the block or through a park with the baby in a stroller. And if sex is a bit less frequent, you may eventually discover that moms and dads share a new intimacy that brings a remarkably high level of relational satisfaction.

Through it all, you'll want to keep open the lines of communication and realize that mistakes will be made and this season won't last forever. Trust that what you're experiencing is all part of God's design. Children are gifts from God, and this new family you're heading up is designed to bring him glory.

"Newborns are mysteries that require a mom and dad working together to solve."

—BROCK GRIFFIN

50

I Want a Divorce

One night, Johnny's wife told him, "I want a divorce." She said she loved him but she didn't want the life they were living. There was a lot missing in their marriage.

Now, this book isn't a marriage manual. But while we think it's great being a dad, we think it's even greater to be a dad raising a family with a healthy, vibrant marriage. So Johnny's story and what he learned in the process is worth a chapter. Wouldn't you agree?

Johnny and his wife were not Christians, but he was desperate, so he went to see a local pastor. That pastor gave him this helpful insight: His wife didn't really want a divorce. She was really saying, "I want a better relationship."

Every marriage has its own unique challenges, but many times the answer is simply a matter of following through on what we intended to do when we got married—serving our spouses, making them a priority, and maintaining romance.

Dad, if you're in a situation like Johnny's, be encouraged. If you choose, you can change your habits and improve your marriage. You can begin right away, but change will take time, and you'll need to demonstrate to your wife that you really are different.

We don't want to oversimplify what it will take, but here are eight quick action points to consider. These may not be new concepts to you, but we all need to hear them once in a while.

- *Make your family top priority* when you're home. Leave work at work and give your wife and children your full attention. Walk in with a smile, excited to see your family.

- *Set date nights* for you and your wife—just the two of you—at least once a month. Get away for a weekend once or twice a year as the budget allows. Do things she loves. Go out just for fun and don't have a personal agenda.

- *Be accountable to other Christian men.* Ask them to check in with you regularly about how your marriage is doing.

- *Communicate.* Make time to really listen to your bride, and learn to open up about what you're going through. She needs that.

- *Write letters* and leave love notes telling her how much you cherish her. Emails and texts are also great ways to let her know you're thinking of her during the day. But there's something special about a handwritten note. Once in a while, include a single red rose or some dark chocolate.

- *Be willing to get help* by attending marriage seminars and seeing a counselor. There's so much good advice available. Ask your pastor for recommendations.

- *Invest in your kids.* Your children need your time and attention. When your bride sees you giving them your all, she feels secure. The image of a dad playing with a toddler can melt the heart of many moms. And when you take the kids, she gets a break.

- *Take steps to grow in your own faith.* Making yourself a better person, a better Christian, is also an investment in your family. Husbands and wives grow closer when they worship and pray together. But your own personal relationship with God is really your top priority for the healthiest, strongest possible marriage.

Dad, don't think of this as a checklist. But if your wife comes to you and says something as drastic as, "I want a divorce," know there are things you can do today for the immediate benefit of your marriage and your family. And if it helps, you can even show this list to your bride and pledge to work on these eight areas of your relationship.

"When a wife has needs, there already exists a man who has accepted the assignment to meet those needs."

—JAY PAYLEITNER

51

The Best Thing

Colin is 11, and he loves tennis. Not long ago, his grandparents were visiting, and they asked if they could watch him play. So Colin and his dad, Brian, got their rackets and took Grandma and Grandpa to the high school courts. They all had a great time.

Later, when Colin was off somewhere else, his dad and grandfather were talking about their tennis excursion. Brian casually said, "Yeah, Colin isn't a natural or anything, but he's getting better. If he works hard, he could be pretty good."

That grandfather's response surprised Colin's dad with a bit of wisdom that speaks volumes. He said, "Yes, but the best thing is that it's something the two of you can do together."

That's a good word for all of us dads.

We certainly encourage you to help your children identify their gifts and excel in different areas of life—sports, hobbies, the arts, and so on. You're probably pretty good at that kind of encouragement. You're helping your son or daughter develop valuable skills and learn life lessons they may not get any other way. You're even willing to spend time and money to give them a chance to reach their full potential.

If they have one-in-a-million talent, heartfelt determination, and a bit of luck, they might make the US Open, play at Carnegie Hall, write a bestseller, grab a gold medal, or reach some other high level of achievement. Maybe they will spread the gospel to thousands or help build God's kingdom in some amazing, unexpected ways. Chasing dreams is one of life's great joys.

But even as they dream, and as you dream right along with them, don't lose perspective. Remember that one of the biggest benefits you can bring to their lives is your presence—just being there, being involved. That strong relationship will give them the confidence and the security to pursue whatever they do in life without having to wonder what you think about them or why you weren't there for this or that.

That perspective will also help you to be a better dad. You don't have to get all bent out of shape about whether your child makes first team or first chair. You don't have to yell at the refs or coaches. You don't have to drive home in a deathly quiet car after a disappointing loss. You don't have to get belligerent or demanding when you're practicing with your child.

In a nutshell, you can apply less pressure and give more encouragement.

Most significantly, the time spent with your child will be filled with joy. The phase of life when you're uncovering your children's gifts and passions really is a great time for dads. In many ways, Colin's grandfather was prophetic. That time together really is "the best thing."

> *"If you give yourself permission to enjoy the experience, this time of helping your kids chase their dreams can be one of the most soul-satisfying seasons of your life."*
>
> **—CAREY CASEY**

52

Dads Are Heroes

Jeff runs a camera for music and drama productions at his church. And in December, he was behind the camera for the kids' Christmas production. His own daughter, Emily, was a member of the cast.

As part of the program, slides came up on the screen showing photos of the kids and some interesting facts about them. Their siblings, favorite color, and all that.

As the program began, Emily's bio came on the screen. Jeff scanned the information and smiled at his daughter's photo and funny answers.

Then he got to the last question: "Who is your hero?" Emily's answer was, "My dad."

Jeff told us he was stunned. He pretty much melted as tears came to his eyes. He had never thought of himself in those terms. He said, "That little one-line response...I had no idea...it changed me inside."

Jeff has always been a great dad. He's involved, he's devoted to his family, and he takes his role seriously. He's committed to passing on a legacy of faith to his kids. He's not the kind of guy to think of himself as a hero. But he *is* a hero to his daughter.

And that's a message you need to hear. You are a hero to your children. They might not admit it; they may not even realize it. But they look up to you, Dad. They depend on you.

You probably aren't a hero like Superman, swooping in to rescue them and then zooming off to another emergency. Actually, you're even better. You're there every single day. And even if you can't see them as much as you'd like, you're still there for them. You're available and willing to serve.

The takeaway idea is obvious. Dad, embrace your superhero identity. Not to puff you up on the outside, but to change you on the inside, like Jeff.

Whatever your fathering role calls you to do or be today, approach it with confidence. Stand tall in your role. Exercise superhuman patience with your children when they get difficult. Display incredible courage when you are called to stand up to culture.

If you want to know what your superhero costume looks like, open up Ephesians 6:10,13-17.

> Finally, be strong in the Lord and in his mighty power...Put on the full armor of God, so that when the day of evil comes, you may be able to stand your ground, and after you have done everything, to stand. Stand firm then, with the belt of truth buckled around your waist, with the breastplate of righteousness in place, and with your feet fitted with the readiness that comes from the gospel of peace. In addition to all this, take up the shield of faith, with which you can extinguish all the flaming arrows of the evil one. Take the helmet of salvation and the sword of the Spirit, which is the word of God.

As you polish your breastplate of righteousness, belt of truth, and helmet of salvation, remember that with great power comes great responsibility. God has a plan for fathers. If you accept the role, God's power really can change you inside. He can make you a heroic father.

"Every kid's first hero is their father. It's up to you to keep earning the title every season of life."

—JAY PAYLEITNER

53

One Thing at a Time

Paul is a great friend of the National Center for Fathering and one of those men who does all he can to help other dads. One evening not long ago, he received a call from an acquaintance who was a young father. This dad had four children and thought he was going to go nuts. He had more challenges than he could handle and didn't know where to begin.

Here's how the phone call went. The young dad would bring up an issue. Paul would ask a few questions to clarify, and then he'd offer a suggestion or two. By the time their conversation was done, they had talked through seven or eight different issues. Paul felt as if he had helped the guy.

A few months later, Paul ran into this same dad at a function, and they talked again. The dad knew Paul had some good wisdom, so he asked five more questions about being a dad, and Paul gave him more ideas and fathering strategies.

When they were just about through, Paul had an insight many of us can learn from. He asked the other dad, "Remember the last time we talked? How many of those other things I suggested earlier have you started on?"

As expected, the young dad answered, "None yet."

Here was an overwhelmed dad. He had asked more than a dozen questions and received solid suggestions from an experienced, caring dad...and hadn't put any into practice. Of course, he was still overwhelmed.

So, what's the point, and what did Paul finally tell him? *One step at a time.* We all have ways we need to improve as a dad. Today there's more advice for dads than ever. Much of it is right on. Take advantage of it. But…work on one thing at a time.

Sometimes you hear about good basketball players who spend the off season focusing on improving the one area of their game they know is weak. Maybe it's an outside shot or a cross-over dribble. Maybe it's simply hitting the weight room to get stronger.

In many ways, it's like that with fathering.

So maybe one of your first tasks is to take an inventory. Determine your weak spots. Search your heart. Think through the last week. Recall conversations and interactions with each one of your children. Get input from your wife. Get input from your kids.

Don't beat yourself up, but decide on an area that needs improvement. Is it listening? Is it knowing your child? Is it following through on promises or maintaining your cool when correcting your kids? Do you struggle to point out positive things to your children along with correcting them? Should you spend more time in prayer? Should you put more effort into your marriage? Does one of your children need a little more focused attention this week or this year? Maybe you simply need to be more patient.

We know a book like this can make you feel as if there's a ton of stuff you need to do. And you know what? There is. Fathering is a huge task with eternal consequences. But we hope you're finding enough encouragement, joy, and rewards to keep you fully engaged and tackling the challenge with gusto.

For now, take our friend Paul's advice. Pick one area, find a way to address it, and make it work.

> *"Seek first his kingdom and his righteousness, and all these things will be given to you as well."*
>
> **—MATTHEW 6:33**

★ ★ ★

54

John and Skyler

Since our launch more than 25 years ago, the National Center for Fathering has been involved in many dramatic stories of real dads connecting with their kids. The heart-wrenching and tragic story of John and Skyler is absolutely the most memorable.

John's wife, Denise, first brought up the idea of John attending a weekend father-daughter event with 16-year-old Skyler. That busy dad thought it was a good idea, and said, "I guess I don't have much time left with her. I'd better do this." Of course, John was thinking about his daughter leaving home in a few short years, but that statement soon took on new meaning.

John and Skyler had a fantastic experience. They had important talks and made commitments to spend more time together in the future. But the very next day, while playing soccer, John suddenly had a massive heart attack and passed away.

Since then, Skyler looks back at their time together with gratitude. As a way to celebrate her father's legacy, she shared her thoughts with NCF. Here's part of what Skyler wrote about that day:

> It was exciting because I am best friends with my mom, and I was getting to be that way with my dad too.
>
> Then Sunday he called before his soccer game just to talk to me. Not my twin brother and me, or my mom, but just me. It made me feel really special to think that that weekend I didn't have to split his attention with my twin

brother. [This was] my chance to have his undivided attention and to connect with him.

In addition to one-on-one time with her dad and that last phone call, one of the priceless gifts Skyler received that weekend was a letter from her dad. He wrote it as part of an exercise during the father-daughter event, and Skyler read it at his memorial service. It's a great example of how dads can affirm their children.

> Skyler,
>
> You probably don't realize how important you are to me because I don't demonstrate my feelings well. I'm amazed at how much you have grown up. People always compliment me on how easy you are to talk with, how much fun you are. They tell me how lucky I am, and I know this too.
>
> I want you to know that I will love you always and want to be involved in your life forever. I want to teach you the life lessons that came hard for me. I will always be available to you to share your successes and your failures—because you can never let me down. You never have to live up to my standards because you have already exceeded them in so many ways.
>
> Thank you for investing this weekend with me. I hope it will be the start of a richer life for both of us.
>
> Love,
> Dad

A few clear messages can be found in the story of John and Skyler. First, the letter from John to Skyler reminds us of the value of blessing your children with words. What a great gift for this girl to hear how special she is to her dad. It's something many children go through their entire lives without getting.

Also, let's give credit to Skyler's mom for encouraging her husband to go on this full-day adventure with his daughter. Just about all dads would be wise to listen to their children's mother when she starts talking about what the kids need from them.

Another takeaway is the value of one-on-one time with your kids. Even if you have a houseful—or *especially* if you have houseful—make an intentional effort to get out with each of your kids on a regular basis. Family time is fabulous, but the best conversations happen when it's just the two of you.

Finally, this is also a good reminder to make the most of organized opportunities to connect with your kids, such as father-son camping trips or daddy-daughter dances. When scout troops, youth groups, park districts, sports teams, and ministries sponsor events or need adult volunteers, be the kind of dad who makes these events a priority.

We believe there should be a sense of urgency about this. Don't put it off. Make sure that when you die—whether it's tomorrow or 50 years from now—your children have many memories of special time with you. You never know how much time you have left with them.

And one more lesson: During the healing process, Skyler found comfort in 1 John 4:16. (Her dad, John, died at 4:16 in the afternoon.) The verse says, "And so we know and rely on the love God has for us. God is love. Whoever lives in love lives in God, and God in them." Dad, we should feel an urgency about sharing that with them too.

> *"Blessings and tragedies come together so often in life. We need to prepare our families for both sides of that equation."*
>
> **—BROCK GRIFFIN**

★ ★ ★

55

Managing Energy Resources

Dads typically think of resource management in terms of finances—providing the home, sustenance, stuff, and security your family needs. Most dads are well aware of that stark reality. It hits you right about the time you buy your first package of diapers. But beyond financial resources, there's a physical resource that a dad should be tracking. It's the energy and stamina he and his children's mother maintain.

Maybe you're a new dad and your baby isn't sleeping through the night yet. Or your toddler is teething, has an earache, or seems to be hungry all the time. Maybe you work long hours, and your kids expect you to play—and play hard—the second you walk in the door.

When the kids grow older, the physical demands on dads change and often diminish. But with young kids, the claims on your energy are nonstop. Young kids don't understand or accept the idea that Dad and Mom might be too tired to play. You feel worn out, and Mom is likely even more exhausted.

If you're both running on empty, you're less likely to do fun activities with your kids. And you're more likely to father from a distance—maybe from a comfortable chair—instead of engaging them where they are and on their level. Even worse, you're also more likely to badger your children or even lose your composure and start yelling at them.

Some dads in that situation even find excuses for spending more time at work. That's a huge mistake. Your time and attention at home are more important than ever.

As a committed father, you need to back away from that dangerous edge. You need to heed the words of Colossians 3:21 (NASB): "Fathers, do not exasperate your children." If it helps, try turning that verse around. "Fathers, be there to support and encourage your family."

Dad, if you and your bride are going through a season in which you are both pretty much always exhausted, it's time to find a workable solution. If Mom is the main caregiver, a wise first step is to come alongside her, appreciate all she does, and take on some of that burden. Make it a new priority to spend one-on-one time with each other away from the kids. At-home moms especially need this.

For yourself, remember that your children deserve a father who's active enough and healthy enough to help them discover and become all that they were created to be. Schedule those regular workouts. Eat healthier. Reduce your stress level. Get the sleep you need. Say a prayer and prepare your heart for fathering excellence as you head home from the job. When you walk in the door, give yourself every chance to be the father your children need.

Dad, managing your physical resources is part of being a good steward of what God has given you. That's part of his plan for your family.

> "Those who hope in the LORD will renew their strength.
> They will soar on wings like eagles; they will run and
> not grow weary, they will walk and not be faint."
>
> **—ISAIAH 40:31**

★ ★ ★

56

Big Ideas

Here at NCF, we are absolute advocates of everyday fathering. Making daily connections. Establishing routines. Being present and consistent in the small, seemingly mundane moments of life, thereby building our children's trust and confidence.

But we also totally applaud big ideas that take weeks of planning, create benchmark moments, and provide an overflow of memories. Two dads gave us some great examples.

Jeff Turner and his son Taylor love to fish. During the summer before Taylor's senior year, the two of them set off on an unprecedented adventure—a quest to fish in all 50 states in 50 days.

The idea began when Jeff realized that college was rapidly approaching for his son. As he said, "I'm just an average father looking at one summer left with my son. What could our adventure be?" The idea actually began about a year before the trip. They spent many hours together researching and preparing for how they could make it work.

Another dad, author Rich Wagner, did something similar with his teenage son. One summer they rode their bicycles across the country, coast to coast, with Mom and little brother following in a van. You know that took a lot of training and preparation as well.

Now, these examples might seem a little extreme. But these two dads saw a chance for a once-in-a-lifetime adventure, and they went for it. The result is something they and their children will never forget. You can't put a price tag on that kind of experience.

Think of the memories the Turner men shared out on a lake in Louisiana or Oregon. Or imagine the Wagners riding up and down the mountain passes of Colorado or across the windy plains of Oklahoma. They faced challenges together when something went wrong or broke down. They leaned on each other for support when the days grew long and frustrations set in. Just thinking about it, we're a little envious. Aren't you?

Worth mentioning, the best part of their adventures might not even have been the adventures! The extra-special father-child bond began with the brainstorming beforehand and will continue with a lifetime of sharing memories.

Dad, even if you don't exactly follow Jeff and Rich's lead, let their examples raise the bar for you. Ask yourself, *What can I do with my child while I have the chance?*

With your teenager, it may take a little thought, a little time, and a little cash. Maybe it's a weekend summer getaway or a missions trip over spring break. Climb a mountain together. Explore a metropolis. Go on an archaeological dig, tour Civil War battle sites, canoe down a canyon, or commit to seeing a half dozen concerts this summer—rock, country, jazz, sacred, or classical.

With your younger kids, it's much easier and cheaper. Camp out in the backyard. Start a collection of pinecones, sea shells, or pretty rocks. Go fishing or explore your local city parks.

Like Jeff and Rich, find motivation in knowing that your time on earth with your son or daughter is not unlimited.

> *"Most men have an adventure they imagined when they were growing up but never embarked on. Children are the perfect excuse for doing it now."*
>
> **—JAY PAYLEITNER**

57

Are You Really Listening?

The National Center for Fathering helps run Father of the Year contests in several states. Not long ago, Matthew Gwynn earned that title in Kansas City.

In an interview with a local newspaper, Matthew's daughter Katie said, "My dad is a very good listener. He will always take the time to listen to my side. I can always talk to him." In a follow-up interview, Matthew confirmed that his best attributes as a father are listening to his children and being active in their lives.

So why is listening so significant for Matthew? *Because he is deaf.* Now, Dad, does that help to expand the definition of "listening" for you?

When we're really listening to our children, we're engaging them with much more than just our ears. With our eyes, we should be looking for facial expressions and nonverbal cues. With our mouths—or hands, in Matthew's case—we should be asking follow-up questions to make sure we understand. With our hearts, we should be tuned in to their feelings about the message they're communicating. With our bodies, we should be demonstrating that we're interested and ready to hear them.

That was also a point of emphasis for Colin Irvine, a Father of the Year in Minnesota. He said that the best parenting advice he ever received was to "bend not at the waist, but instead at the knees." That thought has helped him to slow down, look his children in the eyes, on their level, and show them respect as important people in his life.

Dads like Matthew and Colin understand that when a child comes to you with a problem, many times they're not looking for an answer. Really, they just want you to listen, encourage, and show that you care. Through listening, you can often guide your children to discover solutions themselves.

So when your child comes to ask you something, make a point to put down what you're doing or turn your whole body away from the computer or TV.

Pay close attention even if they're going on and on about something rather trivial. Remember, you want them to keep coming back to you when more important matters are on their mind or weigh heavily on their heart.

Also, we encourage you to ask your family members to rate you as a listener on a scale of one to ten. Then ask, "How can you tell when I'm not really listening?" "How can I do better?" That may sound scary, but becoming a good listener is that important.

> *"My dear brothers and sisters, take note of this: Everyone should be quick to listen, slow to speak and slow to become angry."*
>
> **—JAMES 1:19**

58

Delight in Your Kids

Proverbs 3:12 says, "The LORD disciplines those he loves, as a father the son he delights in."

If you're like most dads, you take that as a reminder to discipline your children. God disciplines us, and we're to follow his example by holding our children accountable for their actions and enforcing consequences for disobedience and rebellion. We do this not because our children get on our nerves, but because we have a higher purpose—to train them to be godly people.

But don't miss the other side of the equation in that proverb. Remember, it says, "God disciplines those he *loves*, as a father the son he *delights* in." In other words, we should make every effort to experience delight and build strong, positive relationships—that's the part that gives balance. Effective fathering immerses those limits in an ocean of love.

Honestly, your efforts at discipline will probably fail if you haven't built a strong relationship with your child. When it comes to changing a child's behavior patterns, negative consequences work well only after you've established a consistent relationship of love and trust. When correcting a child's behavior, positive reinforcement is often more effective than punishment. Negative consequences may be necessary at times, but it's usually preferable to begin most discipline issues with encouragement and validation before resorting to fear or threats.

So, Dad, take delight in your children! You may find that the rules and the issues of the day fall into place quite naturally.

If you haven't already picked up on it, there are hundreds of ways to delight in your brood. Be thrilled the minute your daughter walks in the room. Ask your son to join you out in the driveway for a game of HORSE. Start a water balloon battle or take your child on a late-night trip for ice cream. Noogies. Pillow fights. Stare downs. Knock-knock jokes. Find a way to turn an everyday task into a crazy or fun time with your child—even if it gets a bit messy. Watch videos of your child as a baby to help recapture some of the joy you felt as a father back then. Seek out and share Bible verses about joy and rejoicing.

Dad, be proactive about enjoying your kids—reveling in them and delighting in them.

> *"When a father puts relationships first, the rules become a lot easier to enforce."*
>
> **—CAREY CASEY**

59

Thanks from Tom

At the National Center for Fathering, we feel pretty confident about the words of wisdom we send out for dads. On the airwaves. In the cloud. From speaking platforms and during training sessions. Printed in books. And during one-on-one counseling.

But the wisest words we come across are typically delivered by everyday dads. A dad named Tom wrote to us with some charming and useful insight on loving our kids.

> I want to thank you for your weekly action points. Recently I read in your [email] about how to connect with your small child. [So] I got down on my five-year-old's [level] and told her, "Do you know that I love you wider than an airplane's wings? Do you know that I love you more than Mama kangaroo loves the little baby in her pouch? Do you know that I love you more times than all the leaves on all the trees in our yard?"
>
> Later, she told me with a beaming smile, "Dad, I love when you tell me those things."

The letter went on for a few more paragraphs and ended with words of appreciation.

> Thank you for helping me to make my daughter feel extra special and loved. Those are some of the most special moments in life. Thanks for the encouragement.

Now, here at NCF we kind of wish we could take more credit for Tom's success with his daughter, but it's really just a dad thinking creatively and expressing his heart to his child. If we had a small hand in helping to make that happen, then to God be the glory.

We're sharing Tom's words here because we think there's a nugget you can apply with your children. Ask yourself, *What am I feeling deep in my heart for my child?*

And then, when you sense the pride or love or joy welling up because you have great kids or you grasp the privilege of being a dad, ask, *How can I express what I'm feeling to my kids?* We know it might not happen every day, but if you occasionally pause and reflect on those little people who call you daddy, you are going to experience moments of wonder and deep satisfaction.

Very simply, we encourage you to relay those feelings directly to your child. Why? Tom's daughter said it well. "Dad, I love when you tell me those things."

Too often, we dads don't feel comfortable sharing our emotions, but let's pledge to overcome that. It's not difficult. It's just something you need to decide to do and look for opportunities. Maybe—like Tom—you share a meaningful word picture. Maybe you renew your commitment to spend regular time with your child. Bonus hugs are always a good idea. And every kid wants to hear their dad say, "I thought of you today, and it really felt good."

Thanks for writing, Tom. And we're hoping to hear how other dads show love to their kids. At any age, time, or place. We promise to always be open to any ideas on fathering—including comments, questions, success stories, and even complaints—at fathers.com.

"It isn't that hard to let kids know they are loved, and it will make a huge difference in their lives."

—BROCK GRIFFIN

60

Surprise

Most husbands are smart enough to surprise their wife with flowers once in a while. And it usually turns out pretty well. She's delighted, and you might get a bonus kiss out of the deal. It's a no-brainer.

So...what if you used the same principle with your kids? How might you surprise your son or daughter?

For your daughter, it might indeed be a modest ten-dollar bouquet of flowers. That's not a bad idea at any age.

For your son, it depends on how old he is and what he's into. A plastic dinosaur. A pack of baseball cards. A pack of firecrackers (if they're legal in your state.) A Nerf football.

Other inexpensive ideas include a box of sidewalk chalk, bubbles, a fresh can of tennis balls, or a card game, such as Uno, Mille Bornes, Pit, or Phase 10.

The idea is to surprise your kids for no reason at all. These are not the "Uh-oh" or "Oh, no" surprises. These are the "Ah-ha!" and "Wow!" surprises. Think of them as day brighteners that say, "I'm thinking of you."

Maybe they will be surprised because you haven't been doing all you can as a father, and they'll wonder about the real motives behind your actions. That's okay. Just smile and keep them wondering.

Want other examples? Show up to support your child at an unexpected time and place. Ask questions and show interest in things you haven't talked about before. Anticipate your child's needs and be ready with a secret stash of poster boards, flash cards for the upcoming SAT, or a cold Gatorade at just the right time. Give your first grader a new box of crayons. Fill your teenager's gas tank.

You can also use the element of surprise to break up the routines of life. For no reason at all, offer to take their turn doing the dishes, mowing the lawn, or handling any other regular chore. If they're cramming for finals, surprise them with cocoa, lemonade, or fresh popcorn. If they've just finished a major project or assignment, surprise them with a box of Dilly Bars or Popsicles.

As they prepare for tryouts for the next sports season, surprise them with some new gear, an instructional video, or even some lessons with a coach. Just make sure you don't attach ridiculous expectations to your gift.

Surprises don't have to be things or events. They can be zero-cost reminders that you're thinking about them. What can you text to your son that would bring a smile to his face? What could you write on a sticky note and leave on your daughter's mirror?

You know your kids. You can probably apply this idea in ways we haven't thought of, and we hope you'll do that.

The goal is to keep surprising your family members with good things until they are no longer surprises. You'll suddenly be the husband and father who delights, encourages, and blesses. Instead of the cranky, mean-spirited, and nasty sourpuss you normally are.

> *"Every day, fathers have the chance to delight or to disappoint. Choose wisely."*
>
> **—JAY PAYLEITNER**

61

Coaching Pledge

Sports networks have stumbled onto a formula for grabbing the hearts of their predominantly male viewers: stories of athletes and their fathers.

The Olympic telecasts are a prime example. Producers love to sprinkle human interest stories and shots of family members into the competition footage.

We see dads encouraging and challenging their kids on the sidelines. We watch extended segments showing a dad driving his son to practice early in the morning every day or practicing with his daughter in the backyard or at the gym. When a champion is interviewed, he or she will often mention the father's dedication or how he gave the young athlete confidence to achieve greatness.

Can you imagine your child achieving greatness? You should, because from all appearances, these dads aren't that different from many of us. Plus, they help us demonstrate the Championship Fathering fundamental of coaching.

Like coaches, we fathers don't win medals or get much glory. And rightly so. A coach is focused primarily on helping an athlete reach his or her full potential. So it is with fathers. Our role is to help our children pursue their dreams and to keep giving them a positive vision for what they can be and what they can accomplish.

The ultimate fatherly Coach, of course, is God, our heavenly Father. In Matthew 3:16-17, we read an excellent example of a father blessing his son.

As soon as Jesus was baptized, he went up out of the water. At that moment heaven was opened, and he saw the Spirit of God descending like a dove and alighting on him. And a voice from heaven said, "This is my Son, whom I love; with him I am well pleased."

You've heard that passage before, but did you ever stop to think that from all we can tell, Jesus really hadn't done much of anything yet? God the Father was expressing confidence in his Son even before Jesus started performing miracles and healing people as part of his earthly ministry.

That attitude should be our attitude. Appreciation, encouragement, and love. Even if our kids have not yet gotten their name in the paper.

Dad, you might feel as if people are scrutinizing you when they watch your children. But what your children accomplish isn't about you, so we recommend you just relax and enjoy the ride. Be a good model on the sidelines and choose your words carefully as you talk about the game.

In the end, we should truly focus on what's best for *them* and pledge three important things:

- our consistent support, win or lose;
- our wisdom, based on experience and delivered at the right moments to help them learn from situations;
- and our unconditional love, no matter what.

Whether they win or lose, ride the bench or earn MVP, continue to develop or quit after one season, you can look back and say, "It was a privilege to watch you compete. I'm proud to be your dad."

"Take it from a dad who knows. Don't be the jerk in the stands."

—JAY PAYLEITNER

62

Dads at Weddings

Butch Floyd is a friend of NCF who gave his daughter away in marriage not long ago. In the hours before the reception, the caterer at the athletic club noticed Butch staring out the window during a moment alone. Over the years, she had organized several events for Butch, including business lunches and gatherings for his work with Youth for Christ. But this day—the day he would walk his daughter down the aisle—Butch was revealing his more contemplative side.

The caterer quietly asked Butch how he was doing, and uncharacteristically, his thoughts came tumbling out. Based on their conversation, she wrote a magazine article for the club newsletter that revealed the depth of emotion felt by fathers of brides everywhere.

> Mr. Floyd explained the peace he was feeling at that moment and time and all the prayer that had gone into getting to this day. He told me about his relationship with his daughter, Natalie, throughout the years. She is his "treasure" and turning over his treasure to someone else is something that does not come easily or quickly...He talked about a father's responsibilities in a daughter's life and his role as her father— from the beginning of her life and how they strengthen and grow through the years. He also talked about the process of letting go.

The caterer went on to describe how fathers of the bride typically don't have a lot of input on the details of the reception, but her conversation with Butch helped her realize that those men are still overflowing with hope, emotions, memories, and love.

Hearing about Butch got us thinking about the never-to-be-forgotten moments when our children exchange wedding vows. Carey has been through this experience three times and Jay has seen four sons get married. We've learned that each ceremony and reception will have its own distinct personality, reflecting the bride and groom. In most cases, the role played by the father of a bride or groom is small, and it's almost as if you're watching the event unfold rather than being an active participant. As you look forward to that big day with your child—whether it's a month away or many years—here are some things to keep in mind.

The day is not about you. You know that, but weddings always seem to include issues that cause tension or even major divisions in families. If you have an agenda, put it on the back burner. This is a time to be humble, let others shine, and just enjoy the ride.

Be ready to get involved in the right ways. Be prepared to take any role, whether behind the scenes or a brief moment in the spotlight, such as a walk down the aisle or a dance with the bride. Take on the challenge of making guests feel welcome. One of the best ways to make the day memorable is to find a time to publicly speak a father's blessing on the new marriage. (Speak words of love and humility, but keep it short!)

Be ready to write the check. This is a difficult one because money is a big area where we want our kids to learn responsibility and planning, and their poor money decisions are big learning opportunities. But when it comes to weddings, money can become a big source of disagreement, and it's amazing how much some things cost.

The recommended approach for fathers of the bride and fathers of the groom is to do all you can to *not* let financial stress steal joy from the event. Well beforehand, encourage the young couple to have a budget and plan wisely. But as the big day draws near, if you're able to and if the expenses aren't completely frivolous, be a hero when something unexpected comes up…and do it cheerfully! Be ready with a smile that says, "You're worth every penny."

Remember, Dad, you're helping to make memories that will last a lifetime. And you're setting the stage for continuing a positive relationship with your adult child and welcoming that new son- or daughter-in-law to your family.

> *"Houses and wealth are inherited from parents,*
> *but a prudent wife is from the LORD."*
>
> **—PROVERBS 19:14**

★ ★ ★

63

Expressing Love

At NCF, we know the best fathering ideas are not from us. They're from you. The dads in the trenches. So every once in a while, we put out a call for fresh ideas to meet the needs of dads to reach specific goals. One of our favorite questions is, "How can a dad express love to his kids in simple but creative ways?" We give all the credit for this chapter to the dads who responded.

One dad says he and his kids think of the biggest amount of something to express their love. "I love you more than all the sand on the beach." "I love you more than all the stars in the sky." "More than all the grass on the ground." "More than all the cars on all the roads in the world." And "More than all the toys at Walmart."

Another spin on this is the dad and his kids who try to outdo each other. "I love you from here to the moon and back." "Yeah? Well I love you from here to the moon to the sun and back." "Okay…I love you from heaven, to the stars, back to the moon, and then to the sun, back to heaven a million times, and back." It's always a lot of fun.

Another dad says his daughter often says, "I love you to God and back"—and it can't get any better than that, right? One dad tells his son, "God must love me for allowing me to be your dad."

Then there's the dad who carries out this routine at bedtime with his twin daughters. He starts by saying, "Good night, I love you." Then one girl will say, "I love you too." Dad responds, "I love you three." The counting goes on for a while until the dad finally says, "I love you infinity and beyond." Then one of the girls always says, "Plus one," with a big giggle as the lights dim.

One dad named Jim says he shows love to his kids by yelling at them! No joke. When Tim became a dad, someone explained that kids often misbehave because they want attention, and parents often use their strongest emotions and their loudest words when they're upset—which doesn't help the problem.

So Tim takes the concept to the opposite extreme. When one of his kids brings home a good report card or does something nice, he will often yell at the top of his lungs, "GOOD JOB!" or "THAT'S FANTASTIC!" It sometimes shocks the kids, but when they realize what's happening—that Dad is actually affirming them—they definitely feel the love.

Here's an idea from a creative single dad. He had his own notepads made, using an image he drew with the words "Dad loves" and his daughter's name. This father and daughter write notes back and forth using these custom notepads. That dad uses the same artwork on a special website, on envelopes, sticky notes, pens, and more. Do you think his daughter is getting the message?

Another dad named Paul has heard proof that his expressions of love are getting through. He does quite a bit of camping and boating with his kids, and they often invite friends and cousins. Paul will say things like, "I love you to the moon, to the lake, to the stars, and back." More than once he has heard the young guests say, "Your dad is weird." Paul just smiles.

How do you express love to your crew? Let us know at fathers.com. We'll pass it on to other dads in our books, blogs, and broadcasts. Hey, we're all in this together.

> *"Above all, love each other deeply, because love covers over a multitude of sins."*
>
> **—1 PETER 4:8**

Dads and Sarcasm

So you finally picked up this book for dads and you're two-thirds of the way through. You must be the best dad in the world!

Truth be told, the three coauthors of this book are quite sure that everyone absolutely adores sarcasm. We agree it's one of those wonderful character traits that kids love about their dad and wives love about their husbands. Don't you wholeheartedly agree?

Yikes.

Dad, do you have a sarcastic sense of humor? What would your kids say about the way you talk to them?

Some sarcasm is downright mean—sharp, cutting, and wounding. That's poisonous in families. Sometimes it's hard to believe what parents say to their kids.

More common are the snippy remarks and comments a dad might say almost under his breath. It's not an intentional attack. You might even view it as a harmless little joke or observation, but you would be mistaken.

For example, your eight-year-old son says he wants to do better at helping around the house. And you say, "Oh, like that's gonna happen." Or you're in the van with the whole family and you hear a news story about someone who was dishonest. "Hmm," you say as you tilt your head toward the backseat, "I wonder if we know anyone like that." Maybe your child talks about a new privilege or something special he would like to do. And you say, "Sure…as soon as you get straight

A's"—knowing full well that that's above his abilities. Or your teenage daughter is standing with the refrigerator door open, trying to make a decision. You walk by and deliver a not-so-witty or welcome comment: "More sweets for the princess?"

Maybe your son is short for his age, and you've endowed him with a special nickname to remind him on a regular (and painful) basis. Or your daughter puts on makeup to go somewhere, and you make a comment that includes the word "circus."

We could probably come up with hundreds of examples, but here's the point. Take a hard look at the way you talk to your children, including the comments that you think are harmless. Are they really? We believe that our words carry great power—much more than we realize. And that includes the jokes and passing remarks.

So is there ever a place for sarcasm? Are we making too big of a deal about this?

We're pretty sure those clever little comments accumulate day after day and take a real toll on your children's view of themselves. At the very least, Dad, you're making yourself less fun to be around.

Our recommendation? Sarcasm isn't witty or fun, and it may be destructive. So pull the plug on it and work on building up your children rather than tearing them down. Let the overwhelming message to your kids be that you are thrilled with them and blessed by them just the way they are.

> "Words are perhaps the most powerful tools in a father's toolbox. You can use them either to build up or to tear down. Your choice."
>
> **—BROCK GRIFFIN**

★ ★ ★

65

Get in the Word

What's the biblical foundation for a Christian household?

The third chapter of Colossians contains some pointed direction for Christian families: "Wives, submit to your husbands...Husbands, love your wives...Children, obey your parents." We would encourage you to read and meditate on that entire chapter and see how God might be speaking to you.

Of course, at NCF we often talk about Colossians 3:21—"Fathers, do not embitter your children, or they will become discouraged." We share ways for fathers to avoid embittering their children. That includes positive strategies, such as listening, respecting privacy, loving their mother, and tucking in. And we track fathering habits to avoid, including losing your cool, yelling at referees, and breaking promises.

But there's one more strategy right there in Colossians 3 that we must not overlook.

Backing up just a few verses in that chapter, here's what Paul wrote in verse 16: "Let the message of Christ dwell among you richly as you teach and admonish one another with all wisdom through psalms, hymns, and songs from the Spirit, singing to God with gratitude in your hearts."

Is it going too far to connect that thought to the other statements about how to behave as a husband, a wife, a child, and a father? We don't think so. This concept actually sets up the foundation for how to establish an authentic Christian household. Dad, if we want to do better at being the loving, consistent, encouraging fathers we are called to be, the critical first step is to get in the Word and let it dwell richly in us.

Reading God's Word is the primary way we can discern his will for our lives—and for our fathering. Don't you think that's important enough to devote your time and energy toward learning, studying, and even memorizing the Scriptures?

We hear from dads facing a variety of challenges, and we try to provide them with insights and practical ideas. But looking at this passage from Colossians, maybe there's one answer that faithful fathers need to try first and keep doing over and over. That's right—get in the Word. Let it be a lamp for your feet and a light on your path (Psalm 119:105).

So anytime you ask yourself, *How am I doing as a father?* the next question should be, *How's my daily quiet time going?* We've seen over and over how those two thoughts are surely connected.

Want to be a better dad? Get in the Word.

> "All Scripture is God-breathed and is useful for teaching, rebuking, correcting and training in righteousness, so that the servant of God may be thoroughly equipped for every good work."
>
> **—2 TIMOTHY 3:16-17**

66

The Power of Suggestion

An NCF staff member who shall go unnamed was dining with his wife at a local restaurant. The server brought them water in clear, bulky-looking glasses. Right away he took a drink, and as he set the glass down, he said, "Wow, these glasses are heavy!"

It wasn't true. The glasses appeared to be solid glass but were actually made of plastic and were deceptively light. He was playfully trying to trick his wife—and it worked. She reached for the glass and jerked it up off the table, spilling just a little bit in the process.

That's a lighthearted example of the power of suggestion—the ability to influence others' thoughts and behavior with our words.

That bit of husbandly mischief by our colleague got us thinking about the significant power in the words we speak to our children. Not to oversimplify, but if a father says to a child, "I believe you can do this," that statement increases the chances that the child will succeed in the attempt. How much of an increase? That depends on too many factors to speculate. But even if it increases the success rate by only 1 percent, shouldn't we be using that power for good?

The power of our words can have a chilling impact as well. "You can try that, son, but I'm not sure you're cut out for it." "Why would you want to do that?" "I knew that wouldn't work." "Maybe leave that to someone more experienced (or taller, faster, wealthier, or more level-headed)." With words like that, Dad, we are predisposing our children to take a pessimistic outlook and increasing the chance they will either fail in their attempt or pass up an opportunity altogether.

What if we followed Jesus's example and used the positive power of our words? Remember how he told his followers, "You are the salt of the earth…You are the light of the world" (Matthew 5:13-14). He was calling them to be courageous with their faith.

Praise your kids often. Not with false accolades—children know when your words are insincere. Instead, commit to being aware of their strengths and aptitudes. Notice when and where they have been putting in some extra effort. Assume the best. At the right time, go a little overboard with positive encouragement about something they may want to try. Tell them, "I think you may have found your sweet spot." "I saw how you helped that other boy, and I'm proud of you." "You've got talent. I'm eager to see how God uses it."

Point out skills and God-given gifts as you notice them. Maybe take it a step further and cast a vision of how that gift could turn into a life's calling. When they want to try something new, help them find ways to make it happen. Or tell them how you're praying for their future.

Dad, suggestion is a powerful tool for our fathering. Let's use it to bless and challenge our children to greatness.

> "Therefore encourage one another and build
> each other up, just as in fact you are doing."
>
> —1 THESSALONIANS 5:11

★ ★ ★

67

Father and Son Fencing

Sam Jones is one of our most active master trainers at NCF. In addition to being great in that role, he's also a near-championship fencer. And he demonstrates the qualities of a Championship Father.

For years, Sam has been busy with his son, Stephen, traveling and competing together in fencing. The two of them have participated in major fencing events in the United States and abroad, and both have earned great accolades. Sam himself has placed second nationally in his division, defeating two former world champions in the process.

It's a great story, but for Sam, the best part is the time he and Stephen are able to spend together and how their relationship has grown. As one of them competes, the other one coaches. They practice together, talk strategy, offer encouragement, point out ways they can improve, and celebrate each other's victories.

As Sam said, "The whole thing is [exciting], but the priceless thing [is] me being there with my son."

Perhaps the most inspiring part was how and why Sam got interested in fencing. Years ago, Stephen, in his early teens, first showed an interest in the sport. Where they lived at the time, Stephen was the youngest fencer, and there was no team for kids his age. So Sam joined the fencing club to encourage his son and to learn about the sport. Sam says, "I wanted to help him build up his confidence and let him know he could do it. I wanted to be there to support him 100 percent."

Now, Dad, you may not take up one of your child's interests to the extent that Sam did, battling for the top spot in the nation in that activity. But there are many ways to get involved and support your children, and there are many significant benefits, as Sam's story suggests.

First, your involvement demonstrates your love. Your willingness to stretch a bit, if necessary, to enter your child's world lets them know that they are worth your time and effort and that you place high value on the things they care about. It's a great way to affirm your child.

Second, you get to discover more about your children as they explore new interests and develop abilities and character traits. Just remember that the goal for both of you is *discovery*, not high performance. Accolades and awards are swell but shouldn't be your top priority.

Third, maybe like Sam you'll discover your own gifts or launch into a hobby or sport you never previously considered.

Finally, you get to be there for the victory celebrations and the disappointing defeats. Your presence is extremely valuable in both instances.

So dive in, Dad! Give your son or daughter your 100 percent support in something they love. You just never know where it might lead them—and you.

> *"Extracurricular activities shouldn't divide a family. They should bring dads, moms, and kids closer together."*
>
> **—BROCK GRIFFIN**

68

Lunch with Dad

Grab your calendar and get ready to pencil in a very important date—lunch with your son or daughter.

Think about it this way. You probably make lunch appointments all the time with important clients or work associates. That hour or 90 minutes is essential for you to stay connected with them, get to know them better, assess their most pressing needs, and decipher how you can help meet those needs.

Doesn't your child deserve that same effort and attention?

So pick a date, pick up your child from school, and take them out to lunch. Let them choose the restaurant and the topic of conversation. Of course, if they don't have anything on their mind right away, you can come prepared with a few questions. It doesn't have to be anything deep. The goal is just to carve out some time together and make your kid feel special.

It may be different from your typical workday lunch, but the return on your investment will far outweigh any business deal.

Not sure how to get your child out of school? It's easier than you think. Just call the school office and say, "I'm hoping to take my third grader to lunch." They'll tell you when to pick them up and where. Most schools are surprised and delighted to help fathers be more involved in their kids' lives.

Of course, we should add that another great idea is to have lunch with your child *at the school*. Bring a special treat for lunch or grab a tray and join them in the line. Invite one or two of their classmates to join you.

It really is a blast to hang out with your kids on their turf, and if you thirst for more of that, our WATCH D.O.G.S. (Dads Of Great Students) program was created just for that purpose. Doing lunch is great, but spending an entire day at the school is even better.

Like many of the fathering strategies in this book, you'll want to customize this suggestion for your season of life. But it's one idea that can work for any dad and any kid at any age. Your toddler. Your pre-schooler. Your grade-schooler. Your tween. Your teen. Your college student. Or your son or daughter out in the working world.

Dad, find a day soon for you and your awesome kid to do lunch.

> *"I'm fairly certain that fewer than 1 percent of all kids in your community can say, 'Today I had lunch with dad.'"*
>
> **—CAREY CASEY**

69

Go for It

Here in the twenty-first-century, the media often blurs gender roles, and an organization may even be ridiculed for suggesting that men are different from women. Well, we're going out on a limb to point out a fairly obvious difference between moms and dads. When it comes to slightly dangerous activities, dads are more likely than moms to say, "Go for it!"

We think that's fantastic.

Not long ago, a good friend of NCF named Rolf posted photos from a Girl Scout snow trip on his blog and showed lots of kids and some dads bundled up and smiling as they flew through the snow on a sled or toboggan. And we mean literally flying. Apparently they found a sled run with a nice snow ramp allowing them to catch some air as they rode down. Here's what Rolf wrote:

> As a fully trained Girl Scout leader, I must add a disclaimer that the following activity is not sanctioned by Girl Scouts of America…due to the risk factor involved. This is what happens when dads, after watching too much Olympic snowcross, chaperone [a snow trip]. It was, however, the favorite part of the trip for our little daredevils and, in their words, "awesome."

Adding to Rolf's words, we just want to say…Dad, take note. Your kids need to see your fun-loving, adventurous spirit. Sure, moms can be daredevils too, and we hope many of those Girl Scouts grow up and take their own sons and daughters on a wild toboggan run someday. But truthfully, we also know that quite a few moms would shake their heads at the photos Rolf posted. Those pics were inspiring, impressive, and pretty close to foolhardy. Let's just say we're kind of surprised no bones were broken.

At this point, on behalf of the National Center for Fathering, we should also provide a disclaimer. But sometimes the fun and the adventure are worth a little bit of risk.

Why? Because that's what dads do! That's one way we build unique bonds with our children.

Now, does this mean we always know what's best for our kids, and we should never listen to our children's mothers when they tell us to be more careful? Absolutely not. We are part of a parenting team. Kids need to be nurtured and kept safe. Kids also need adventure and healthy risk-taking. Parents need to work together, go with their strengths, and model all these character traits to raise well-rounded adults.

Worth emphasizing, there will always be applause for gutsy moms and for nurturing dads. As partners in parenting, let's vow to look for opportunities to develop both sides of that equation with our kids.

Worth double emphasizing, research shows children grow and benefit from occasional adventurous activities. In most cases, a good thrill ride, some whooping and hollering, and a few bumps and bruises are all part of a healthy childhood.

As Rolf suggests, kids have a great time in the process. And we're pretty sure you will too!

> "When two parents watch their child climb a tree, the first
> one to say, 'That's high enough' is almost always mom."
>
> **—JAY PAYLEITNER**

70

24/7/365

Deuteronomy 6 is a great place to learn about leading your children to faith in Christ and trusting God in all things.

> These commandments that I give you today are to be on your hearts. Impress them on your children. Talk about them when you sit at home and when you walk along the road, when you lie down and when you get up. Tie them as symbols on your hands and bind them on your foreheads. Write them on the doorframes of your houses and on your gates (Deuteronomy 6:6-9).

When you read this passage, it's easy to get excited about all the opportunities we have to impress godly values on our kids. But don't get ahead of yourself. The first line of this passage confirms that God's commandments are supposed to be upon our own hearts first. That's critical because so much of leading our children spiritually is about the Championship Fathering fundamental of modeling. If they see God working in us, life with him becomes real. If they don't see it, we have become obstructions to their spiritual growth.

Once we establish our own personal faith and trust in the God of the universe, we can move ahead and impress those things on our children. That's also a great word that might be skipped over. *Impress*. It conjures up images of a gentle yet firm influence worth striving for. We can't hit our kids over the head with the gospel. But we also can't just leave our beliefs sitting around and hope our kids pick up on them. As the passage dictates, you need to "impress them on your children."

The next verse highlights the informal aspect of this process. Structured devotions are valuable, but we also need to emphasize a daily walk of faith, talking about God's plan when we sit at home and when we walk along the road, when we lie down and when we get up.

Then we're directed to surround ourselves with reminders—on our hands and foreheads, on our doorframes and gates. We need daily reinforcement because we live in a world where most of the things we see and hear distract us from living godly lives. If that's a challenge for us, we know it is for our children also.

So let's summarize this remarkable passage for parents with a reminder and a challenge. Training our children in God's commands is not a one-day thing. It's an everyday thing—a natural part of life. We need to own our own faith and accept the responsibility to be intentional about leaving that legacy.

We can't just sit back and expect it to happen. We have to carve out time, build stronger relationships, and have a plan to pass on important truths and values. We can't settle for the ways of the world; we want to keep the Lord at the forefront at all times.

We urge you to talk with your children's mother and come up with a specific plan that is in play 24/7/365. We trust this book is a helpful part of that plan. NCF has other resources, but don't limit yourself to our website and services. Plug into the youth and children's ministry at your church. Talk to other godly parents. Make regular trips to your local Christian bookstore. And spend time in daily prayer for your ongoing ministry to those kids whom God has placed in your care.

> *"Pass on truths in the routines of life. During TV commercials. In the car. Strolling down a dirt road. Tucking in bed. Chatting over waffles. Dad, make it an ongoing conversation."*
>
> **—JAY PAYLEITNER**

71

Start Simple

Quite a few dads grew up in church, but as they graduated high school and moved on with their life, it became less of a priority. Sundays were days to sleep in or relax. With a schedule jam-packed with obligations and distractions, it became increasingly difficult to sit through a long sermon. And who really wanted to think that hard anyway?

Many of these guys got married in a church building with all the trimmings and trappings, but that didn't really jump-start their faith either. Their wedding day was actually more focused on the reception than the ceremony.

But when a little baby comes along, something happens. Suddenly these new dads realize that life doesn't revolve around them. They have responsibilities beyond their own needs. Right in their home is a little person who represents the future. Suddenly they gain an eternal perspective and begin to experience big-picture thinking.

That spiritual awakening triggers two significant realizations. First, new fathers often feel the need to connect or reconnect with God themselves. And second, they feel a heightened sense of responsibility to instill some kind of faith in their children.

That's one of God's gifts to fathers. Being a dad helps us take life a little more seriously. Our new title and accompanying responsibilities force us to consider where our lives are going. Maybe you are one of those men who didn't think much about going to heaven until you were holding a baby and wondering what was ultimately in store for that child.

But then the questions start to come. *What now? Where do I start? How can I possibly pass along a personal faith when I'm not plugged into God myself? I had a Bible…where did I see it last?*

These guys don't feel adequate to lead their children in spiritual things. They don't feel as if their own spiritual walk is where it needs to be. Even if they feel close to God, they know they can't measure up to the teaching of other Christian leaders.

If any of that describes you today, Dad—whether you're a new dad or you've been at it for many years—we have an encouraging word for you: It's best to *start simple* when it comes to your child's faith. Your commitment and follow-through makes a bigger difference than your deep spiritual lessons.

In John chapter 3, Jesus was talking to Nicodemus, a grown man who was having trouble understanding the idea of being born again. So Jesus schooled him up. He made a simple yet deeply profound statement that has become probably the best-known verse in the Bible. New believers, young children, and even desperate dads can understand and memorize John 3:16: "For God so loved the world that he gave his one and only Son, that whoever believes in him shall not perish but have eternal life."

Many people seem to think faith is a strange and complicated thing. But Jesus boiled it down and made it simple and direct. Faith is about belief and trust. Begin there, Dad. That's a fine foundation on which to build your legacy of faithful service and giving glory to God.

For sure, there is a time and place for more involved theological discussions with your kids. Those will come. Hebrews 5 tells us that believers need to grow up and eat solid food—they can't just drink milk all their lives.

But for now, it's a good idea to start simple. If you feel unprepared or unqualified to lead your children, we want to take the pressure off.

Give your children just enough to digest today. As you grow in understanding and spiritual maturity, they will too. Eventually you'll enjoy comparing notes on the meaning of a certain passage of Scripture or a sermon illustration used by a favorite pastor.

> *"One of the greatest turning points in a man's spiritual development is the day he becomes a father because he suddenly realizes how much he is loved by his heavenly Father."*
>
> **—CAREY CASEY**

72

A Stepfather's Breakthrough

A stepdad wrote to us with a heavy heart. Chris just wasn't connecting with his teenage stepdaughter and was hoping someone at the National Center for Fathering could help. His letter explained how he was devoted to his stepdaughter, Emma, but she didn't include him in things, and when he told her "I love you," she didn't respond in kind.

This stepdad went on to say that the two of them weren't necessarily adversaries, but Chris wanted more for their relationship. Plus, he confessed, they recently had an argument and hadn't spoken for several days.

Well, the person who responded to Chris was actually a stepmom—the wife of one of our staff members. And she shared a few key thoughts.

First, as a stepfather, you have to adjust your expectations. It may take quite a while to bond with a stepchild. Sometimes your efforts won't bear much fruit until the child is an adult.

Also, accept that being a stepfather is a selfless job—even more than raising birth children. It's all about giving, and sometimes there's no getting in return. Focus on ways you can invest in your stepchildren and enhance their life, and know you're being obedient to God regardless of what comes back your way.

Finally, don't forget to lean on your spouse and other parents you know. Share your struggles and encourage each other to keep going even in hard times.

Now, here's what happened when Chris received our response. First, he said, it helped just to know he's not alone. Then he started thinking less about what his stepdaughter wasn't doing and more about what he could do to make things better. He realized he had behaved like a child, and he owned a lot of the blame for this latest argument. Chris decided he wanted to make things right.

Emma was at school, which meant he couldn't call her right away. He sent her a text: "Emma, I will tell you later in person, but I apologize for losing my temper. I love you."

Within half an hour, he received a reply: "I love you too."

That evening was Emma's first volleyball game of the year. The girls were warming up when Chris and his wife walked into the gym. Emma saw them and ran over to give him a big hug, and Chris's eyes filled with tears.

Chris knows he still has much work to do. But he has a new resolve to love his stepdaughter with selflessness, patience, and humility. If you're a stepdad, we hope the same for you.

> *"A stepfather is a man of courage who steps in and makes sacrifices for kids he loves even though they may not yet love him back."*
>
> **—CAREY CASEY**

73

Playing Fair

Some guys respond to conflict by withdrawing or simply avoiding confrontations. Others do the opposite—they explode or lose control and damage those around them.

You might not think about this a lot, but handling conflict is an important responsibility for fathers. Our family members often take their cues from us—our actions can inflame a situation or lead to resolving it.

Since so many dads struggle with how to handle conflict, we're always on the lookout for strategies for reducing anger and controlling our emotions. On our shelves at NCF, we have some big, thick books on the topic written by famous psychologists and respected theologians.

But not long ago one of our staff members saw a sign on the playground at his children's elementary school. It listed seven strategies for playing fair. We think they just might apply to men facing conflict. See if you agree.

1. Listen. By listening, you avoid flying off the handle, and you're also more likely to handle the situation without the misunderstandings that almost always makes things more difficult.

2. Talk it over. Once again, too many conflicts are based on not really understanding each other. Make sure you express your concerns without blaming or a lot of wild emotions.

3 and 4. Share and take turns. In other words, think about the other person's perspective and be willing to compromise. Work toward a win-win solution.

5. Apologize. This is a big one for dads. Apologies must include sincere words and more. Show that you truly do regret what happened and you want to do your part to make things better.

6. Walk away. The Bible teaches us not to let the sun go down on our anger, and that's God's will for us. But that doesn't always mean we have to solve every issue right away. Sometimes, because of heated emotions or other reasons, it's good to agree to take a break and talk more later.

7. Get help. Sometimes you need an outside perspective or more qualified expertise to help get past a sticking point in a relationship. We don't want to minimize or oversimplify the challenges of being a man who loses his temper. If you walk through the first six principles and still find yourself experiencing moments of uncontrollable rage, find the courage to take the next step, which may include talking to a counselor or pastor.

Are you wrestling with internal conflicts and huge decisions? Maybe you just need to take a breath and think back to the things you learned in elementary school.

And further, if you can teach your kids to use these skills, they may avoid a lot of the troubles many of us went through.

Make sense, Dad? Now play fair. And play nice.

> *"The solution to our biggest challenges might be articulated with simple, unequivocal words. Listen. Talk. Forgive. Believe. Trust."*
>
> **—JAY PAYLEITNER**

74

Tyler's Column

A student named Tyler wrote a column for his college newspaper. He began by saying, "My biggest fear is twofold. I'm afraid that one day I'll grow up to be just like my father. And I'm scared to death that I'll never be anything like him." He continues, "But right now…we barely understand each other."[3]

The column was written after a slightly tumultuous trip home for Thanksgiving and was prompted by Tyler's anticipation of the coming three weeks he would be home for the holidays. He knew getting past the typical frustrations and conflicts would require some extra effort.

If you're reading this today as a father of a young adult—or you're a young adult yourself—maybe some of this is hitting home. Fathers during that stage are reflecting on the past and figuring out how to relate to their kids as adults. For the kids, it's very clear that Dad has some imperfections, but at the same time, they usually know they need to depend on him in important ways.

We want to give Tyler a lot of credit for understanding the important role fathers play. He writes, "Our relationships with our fathers determine a lot about who we are…I might go so far as to say that our relationships with our fathers is the most important relationship we'll ever have. If he loves us well, we'll feel secure. But if he loves us poorly, we'll search for his attention somewhere else, finding it where we can."

More and more, Tyler is seeing ways he is like his father. And though his dad can be tough to love, Tyler loves him still.

For Tyler, recognizing his father's influence is a big step toward less frustration and more understanding between them.

If your kids are young adults, we encourage you to give them freedom to express their emotions and even their frustrations about you as a father. Engage your maturing son or daughter in a dialogue, and show respect for their perspective.

Going forward, show your children kindness however you can—even if you disagree on some issues. Connect with them as adults. Encourage them. Meet some of their needs—not to bail them out of bad decisions, but with the goal of helping them better establish their independence. Let them know that you will always be their dad and that you consider it an honor and privilege.

When things settle down and they think about your role and all you've done for them, like Tyler, your children will come around and learn to appreciate you all the more.

> "Dads should expect and even look forward to some conflict as their young adult children prepare to head off into the world on their own. It's all part of establishing their independence. That's the goal, right?"
>
> **—CAREY CASEY**

★ ★ ★

75

The Father-Child Getaway

Family outings and events are great. Do them often. Whatever size family you have, make the effort to get the entire crew together on a regular basis. As the kids get older, time is more precious, and family times become harder to schedule. But there's great satisfaction in watching your kids interact with each other. Sharing, competing, talking things out, and building forever bonds.

With that said, we can't overstate the importance of a dad and a child heading off for an intentional, fun, and memorable long weekend. Just two of you. Dad and son. Dad and daughter. It's an entirely different dynamic. One-on-one time with a child allows you to learn more about each other, experience life, and make unique memories.

It doesn't have to be all that expensive. Since there's only two of you, the costs don't add up quite as fast as they do on big family trips. Over a long weekend you could spend time practicing a sport your child enjoys or go to a museum or hall of fame that reflects their interests. Go back to nature. Camp out. Go rock climbing or fishing. Visit a big city and try something new together. Like sushi. Or the opera. Rent bikes or canoes. Or rent a couple of those two-wheel Segway contraptions. Hit the art galleries.

Don't overlook opportunities presented by your local park district, church, or family-centered ministries. The National Center for Fathering and many other national organizations sponsor retreats and events for fathers and kids.

In the moments when you're resting from all the activity, you'll be blessed with opportunities for uninhibited conversations about life, temptations, relationships, sex, your child's spiritual walk, future aspirations...those kinds of things.

The idea is quantity one-on-one time with your child. Making this a priority will communicate that you place high value on them. You'll also discover that *quantity* time together will almost always create moments of priceless *quality* time with your child.

You might be thinking, *Sounds good, but I can't take an entire weekend away.* We hear you. You've presented a legitimate argument. But we'd like to counter that point. Your son or daughter will never be this age again. It's now or never.

So grab your calendar. Pick a three-day weekend. Or any three days. We don't often recommend missing school, but this idea is that important.

Let your child help choose the location, and brainstorm about what fun things you can do there. Start thinking and planning now, Dad. This can be a touchpoint moment. Your son or daughter will talk about their weekend with dad for the rest of their lives.

"Quality time with your children first requires quantity time."

—CAREY CASEY

76

Freedom in Accountability

A man we'll call Eric fell into a sinful habit of using pornography. His wife discovered it and was devastated. Things were going downhill fast when they contacted Paul, a friend of NCF who works in men's ministry and marriage counseling.

Paul agreed to meet with the couple, but right away things seemed hopeless. Eric and his wife were distant and had very little motivation to try making things better. So Paul talked with Eric separately. He got him to admit his pornography habit was not a small problem and talked him through steps to address it.

One of the most important steps was to get Eric to tell another man about his struggles. Paul asked Eric, "Who's your best friend? That's the person you need to call *today* and talk to."

Of course Eric resisted the idea at first, but he finally made a commitment to call his friend. As soon as he made the call, Eric found out what a good friend he had. That other man pledged to help him in any way he could. He set up regular meetings for accountability and even started calling Eric throughout the week to check in.

The next time Eric talked with Paul, he sounded like a different man. "I can't believe the freedom I have, even after just a few days." All because he told a friend who could be there for him and vice versa. He has accountability; he's protected. And he's now working through things with his wife.

We need to have very close and open relationships with our brides.

But whatever situation you're in, sometimes it takes another man to really understand where you are and to restore optimism and hope to your life.

We know Satan doesn't like this kind of behavior. He doesn't want you to tell anybody about your issues or your weaknesses. You're more vulnerable when you go solo. He'd rather have you wallowing in self-pity and feeling defeated and hopeless.

But God gives us power through fellowship and confession to overcome our challenges. James 5:16 tells us, "Confess your sins to each other and pray for each other so that you may be healed."

Dad, whether your struggle is similar to Eric's or totally different, open up to a trusted friend and get that help and accountability—and freedom. As dads, we need to work together and help each other to be the men and fathers God has called us to be.

> *"There's a bit of irony in the idea that one of the secrets to self-empowerment is realizing you don't have to go it alone."*
>
> **—JAY PAYLEITNER**

★ ★ ★

77

Trial or Blessing?

Rob is a veteran dad, fiftyish, and the father of a special-needs child. Sharing with a group of dads, he made a startling statement. The men were talking about being sensitive to their children and their needs, and Rob said, "I wish all of you could have the gift of a Down syndrome child. It's been such a blessing for our family, and more than anything else, it has helped me become more aware, more tuned in to my kids."

He added that the experience has also changed his family interactions for the better. His other children have become more perceptive about the needs of their siblings and other people around them, and they are more willing and able to jump in and help someone else when they see a need. They are better people because they are part of a family going through unusual circumstances.

We're pretty sure Rob wouldn't wish any difficulties on any other dads, and we wouldn't either. On the other hand, who determines what is a difficulty and what is a blessing? Do we look just at our own convenience? Or should we try to see things more from God's perspective—where life isn't about pursuing instant happiness, but rather long-term holiness?

That goes for our kids too. Maybe the best circumstance to help them become more Christlike isn't a life where everything works out great and there are no challenges. Maybe dealing with unexpected surprises and trials is the best way to grow—for us and for our children.

Meeting challenges also prepares us to help others who may need to face similar challenges.

Maybe that's the thought behind James 1:2: "Consider it pure joy…whenever you face trials of many kinds."

At NCF, we have great admiration and respect for dads who have special-needs children and step up to the challenge, even finding great joy and purpose in the journey.

In the same way, we urge you to coach your children in this area. When they complain because they're going through something they perceive as a trial, help them see a different perspective and challenge them to step up and meet the task head-on. Going back to James 1, those experiences help us to grow in perseverance and to become "mature and complete, not lacking anything" (verse 4).

Who wouldn't want that for his children? Thanks, Rob, for your example, this reminder, and your willingness to share this idea with other men.

> *"During a victory celebration, dad is the guy who stands in the background giving honor to his wife, credit to his kids, and glory to God."*
>
> **—BROCK GRIFFIN**

78

Wiser Discipline Strategies

Dads are getting more and more creative in their discipline techniques. One dad made news when he shot a hole in his teenager's laptop. Another had his daughter stand on a street corner with a sign that said, "I sneak boys in at three a.m. and disrespect my parents." Another dad wanted to make sure his daughter got the message about the proper length for jean shorts, so he made his own pair of short shorts and wore them when the two of them went to play miniature golf.

For the record, we're not endorsing any of these discipline ideas. Especially embarrassing your kids in public. But we sure appreciate those dads for taking action.

As an alternative, we'd like to offer four guiding principles when it comes to discipline issues and correcting your kids.

Don't make it about you. Many dads struggle in this area, including just about all the dads working at NCF. When a situation comes up with our kids, we might be more concerned about getting some peace and quiet, putting the child in their place, or maybe even asserting our own right to be in charge. But those things are more about what we feel than what is best for our kids.

Use consequences to teach your child. Sometimes they won't learn unless they lose a privilege or their life gets much harder for a day, a week, or longer in some cases. Natural repercussions that happen as a result of a negative choice will get their attention and can have powerful results. Consequences also prepare them for the real world, where irresponsibility and disrespect will cost them in very real ways.

Don't embarrass or humiliate—even as a last resort. It's okay to show some emotions; often it's good for a child to see that you're disappointed, sad, or even angry because of what they've done. Just make sure those emotions don't lead you to go too far.

Stay positive. Keep your ultimate, big-picture goal in mind—to help your child learn and grow from their mistakes. Everything you do should be about that. Even in correction and discipline, our children should come away from the experience knowing, *Dad loves me. He's doing this because he wants the best for me.*

> "No discipline seems pleasant at the time, but painful. Later on, however, it produces a harvest of righteousness and peace for those who have been trained by it."
>
> **—HEBREWS 12:11**

★　★　★

79

Doing Your Fair Share

Not long ago, a survey polled married moms about sharing household responsibilities with their husbands. Reuters reported on the survey and included this attention-grabbing bullet point: "Both Working and Stay-at-Home Moms Feel like a 'Married Single Mom.'"[4]

The image is a bit startling. The survey revealed other findings also worth our attention: 92 percent of working moms and 89 percent of stay-at-home moms feel overwhelmed by work, home, and parenting responsibilities. Seventy percent (working) and 68 percent (at-home) of moms feel resentful toward their partner because of the unbalanced load of household and parenting responsibilities. Eighty-four percent of stay-at-home moms don't get a break from parenting after their partner walks in the door at night, and 50 percent say they *never* receive a time-out from parenting.

As you might guess, that survey drew some criticism for being biased or unreliable and for undervaluing a dad's role as a provider. If you feel offended or taken for granted when you hear this, that's okay. But there's no doubt some dads act like playmates, caring for the kids only when they feel like it or when they have extra time. What's more, let's admit that when some dads finally pitch in and take care of their kids, they act as if they deserve an award for making sacrifices above and beyond the call of duty.

Regardless of how you're doing in this area, we would encourage you to dig a little deeper into how well you're working as a team with your bride and whether you're doing your fair share. Don't wait for looks of exasperation or desperation from your child's mother. Be pro-active.

If you have the courage, ask your bride, "Do you feel overwhelmed?" If she says yes, ask, "How can I help?" Get specific about household tasks you could take over. Maybe you'll be in charge of driving the kids to school, grocery shopping, and after-dinner cleanup. Consider making arrangements for one morning, one afternoon, or an entire day *every week* when your bride can do her own thing. That might mean hiring a nanny once a week, enlisting grandma's help, or readjusting your own schedule.

In 1 Peter 3:7, husbands are instructed, "Be considerate as you live with your wives, and treat them with respect." If our wives express feeling frustrated or overwhelmed with all that's on their plates, our first step should not be to defend our approach or stand up for our right to be the way we are. As servant leaders, it isn't about us.

Our first response should be to understand what our wives are going through and own up to whatever we have brought to that situation. Then we can work out a plan to make things better.

In other words, let's do our fair share. And maybe even a little more than that.

> "When it comes to division of duties, there's still mom stuff and dad stuff, but more and more responsibilities are falling under the category of parenting stuff."
>
> **—BROCK GRIFFIN**

80

Your Dad's Obituary

This chapter is a bit different from the others. It's a personal experience told from the viewpoint of just one of the coauthors.

My father passed away not too long ago, and the funeral director offered to write the obituary. Well, I'm a writer, and the topic was my dad, so I figured I should take a crack at it. It was quite an experience.

Ken Payleitner was a World War II vet, an elementary school principal for 32 years, and a loving patriarch to his family of four children, eleven grandchildren and two great-grandchildren. Ken and Marge were married 61 years. Those are the bare facts. At first, I thought that was all that needed to be said.

But then I started digging. Digging up stories from old students and teachers—stories I had never heard before. Then, searching my own memory bank, I recalled how my dad had always been there at critical junctions in my life—educational, career, and spiritual turning points—often helping transform occasions of disappointment into opportunities for growth.

The final draft turned out to be about twice as long as most obituaries. Most of what I uncovered never made it into the newspaper. In any case, the process was tremendously valuable for me and my entire extended family as we prepared for the wake and funeral.

As I stood in line at the funeral home shaking hands, I found myself looking into the eyes of scores of people who said, "Your father was a wonderful man," "Your dad was important to me," and similar statements. Because I had a chance to reflect on my dad's life ahead of time, I could better understand what all those people were saying. I could smile through the tears.

As a son, you may be called to write your own father's obituary or at least provide background for it. What will you say? Regardless of what has gone before, one of your privileges and responsibilities is to honor him as a father and perhaps to lift up all fathers in the process. By honoring him, you're also connecting the generations—from your father to you to your kids and your grandkids. There's power in family.

Of course, the entire process became one last challenge from my dad to me—a challenge to work even harder on my own legacy, my own obituary. What will my sons and daughter say about me?

Which leads me to ask you the same question. When the time comes, what will be remembered and written about you? If that thought makes you uncomfortable, I recommend you start working on a plan that will add a few positive paragraphs to your obituary ASAP.

For me, the whole process of thinking about the arc and impact of our lives culminated in an entire new book project. I ended up writing *What If God Wrote Your Bucket List?* at the same time we were working on this book.

The most significant reflection for all dads is the way our life is impacting others—friends, coworkers, neighbors, and especially our kids.

Finally, if you're secure in your relationship with God and his Son, Jesus, this chapter really isn't as morbid or depressing as some people might think. The funeral of a decent man who realized his need for a Savior and accepted that free gift of grace is really a beautiful thing.

"What if God wrote your bucket list?"

—JAY PAYLEITNER

Media Madness

What do you do when the latest movie, music download, TV show, or video game is out, and your child is begging to check it out? And what if it has a rating or reputation that makes you question whether it's appropriate? Here are some guiding principles that you can apply to most forms of media.

Be involved. Listen to the lyrics. Research the video game. Sit down and watch an episode of the show. See the movie. (Maybe right alongside your son or daughter.) Find out for yourself what's really in this hot new release and don't judge too quickly. You can learn a lot from online resources that provide detailed reviews for parents. Take what you find out and measure it against the biblical values and principles that drive your family.

Have a conversation and ask questions. Using the information you've gleaned, your involvement should include a dialogue with your child (not a monologue). What appeals to them about the movie, show, or game? Extend your child respect by listening first and giving them some benefit of the doubt.

Talk about some of the themes that are prevalent and the real-life consequences that go with them. For example, depending on the movie, you might discuss oppression and injustice, courage and bravery, responses to authority, or overcoming obstacles. Is the plot making a point about violence, or love, or the roles of men and women? What comment is it making about today's world? Ask your kids, "Where is

God in this?" Or "How would faith make a difference for that character?"

Address concerns. When it comes to video games, you will very likely express concern about excessive violence, and your son or daughter will respond, "It's not real. It's just a game." That gives you a chance to talk about the impact of what we put in our minds and how images and impulses repeated over and over condition and desensitize us, becoming part of who we are.

Remember, Dad, these media challenges with our kids are bonding and coaching opportunities. Issues that might seem difficult or negative can often become teachable moments for the future. If you look for them, these opportunities happen just about every day. You don't have to wait for the next blockbuster to hit the theaters or the release of the next music download.

Make sure you don't get distracted from or bored with the process of shaping your child. Finding teachable moments should be at the core of your fathering game plan; it's a routine part of life.

Know your child. No matter what rating is stamped on a movie or game, every child is unique. Not every 13-year-old is the same. Is your child deeply moved by on-screen drama? Are they always mindful of the difference between fact and fiction? Are they watching and playing for fun, or are they flirting with an obsession? Would they understand the difference between necessary violence and gratuitous violence? Would certain scenes or images haunt them, or would they be able to leave them in the theater or set them aside when the gaming system is turned off?

Your child's mom will have an opinion on this. Do everything you can to get on the same page with her. But this might be an area where you can take the lead. Protect your family. But also don't overreact and ban every media influence from your home. That will almost always end poorly.

Come alongside your children—literally—and help them make

wise decisions. The better you know your child, Dad, the better you'll be able to have a positive influence on specific media challenges that come along. Your influence and your voice will be heard even when you're not around.

> *"Examine everything carefully; hold fast to that which is good; abstain from every form of evil."*
>
> **—1 THESSALONIANS 5:21-22** NASB

82

Roles of a Forever Father

During a recent Father of the Year essay contest, a dad named Alan described his relationship with his kids this way: "Part companion, part playmate, part teacher, part pastor, part chef, part butler, part judge and jury, part dart-gun target, part coach, and forever father."

It's reminiscent of some of the tributes we see around Mother's Day, where moms are described as having all those different roles—doctor, psychologist, maid, teacher, taxi driver, and so on. Moms are great at all of that, and they deserve to be recognized. This isn't a competition, but dads wear many hats too, and Alan has a great take on it.

So how would you describe your role in your children's lives? You might choose some different words here and there, but the point is that we have all kinds of connection points with our kids. Some of those roles may be out of our comfort zone, but that shouldn't stop us from doing what our children need.

Are you your children's companion? Do you often just hang out? Are you investing quantity time, knowing that quality time will often grow out of it?

Are you a playmate? That one comes naturally for many dads, so just go with it.

What about a teacher? In some families, Mom is the main homework general, and in others it's Dad. Getting involved in our children's education goes a long way toward setting them up for success at school, which can be a huge advantage going forward.

Here's one many dads find challenging: pastor. Are you purposeful about nurturing your children in their faith—leading family worship and prayer times? This may be a role that easily gets shoved aside when life gets busy, but it may be the most important of all. I hope you'll recommit to it as a priority.

There's Dad as chef and butler—doing your role in daily child care and household duties. As a judge-and-jury dad, you need to have a plan for discipline and work with Mom to train your kids to be responsible. How about dart-gun target? There's another nod to the fun-loving, playful dad.

One obvious title is coach. You might coach your kids in sports or other pursuits, but your coaching can apply to all of life as you gain insights about what your children need and then help them reach their full potential.

Mentioning the last role you play may get you thinking in a whole new way about the relationship of fathers and their children. Somewhere down the road you might be a dependent. That's right, Dad. Just as you pour out your heart taking care of their every need, a few decades from now you may be totally dependent on their care of you. And that's not a bad thing. Because you've given so much to your kids, that season of life won't be as difficult as you think.

So keep fulfilling your many roles with creativity, compassion, and courage. Proudly own the title of forever father.

> *"The roles of a forever father are forever changing."*
>
> **—CAREY CASEY**

83

Don't Be Surprised

Doug is a friend of ours at NCF and a very committed and involved dad. Not long ago, he sent us a note after going on a field trip with his son's kindergarten class.

Doug said that there were more than thirty kids, two teachers, and four parents along for the ride, but he was the only dad or father figure that day. He said that overall, it was a great time—the kids and teachers enjoyed having him there, and he had fun too.

As it turned out, Doug found himself keeping track of some of the more energetic and troublemaking kids. He didn't mind much, but as the day went on, he said it was obvious how much those kids craved attention from a male role model. They gravitated to him, asking questions and hanging around to see what he would do or say. All the kids, not just Doug's son, really ate it up.

On the bus, they drove by an apartment complex, and one boy said proudly: "My dad lives there, in that apartment. That's *his* place." Doug said it was a nice moment but also a bit sad because it was clear this boy didn't get to see his dad as often as he wanted to.

For that day, those kids had a father figure. Doug saw it firsthand, and he also saw the need to challenge other dads to get involved in the same way. We couldn't agree more. Committed dads like Doug should make every effort to plug in at their child's school, whether it's for lunch, a field trip, or a whole day at the school as a WatchDOG dad.

We hope you'll do that, Dad. But even more than that, we want to encourage you in a big-picture kind of way. Wherever you are, whether it's at your child's school, at church, in your neighborhood, a youth sports event, or somewhere else, this kind of thing will happen to you too. Kids who need a dad will gravitate toward you.

So here's the point. Do not be surprised! You should probably even expect those kinds of things to happen and be ready. You have father power whether you realize it or not, and a lot of kids are hungry for it. Maybe God has placed you in that situation to speak hope and encouragement to a child who needs what you can give.

> *"Any dad who isn't sure how to connect with his kids might consider doing what moms do."*
>
> **—JAY PAYLEITNER**

★　　★　　★

84

Poop, Pee, and Carrots

Little seven-month-old Enoch has a rare genetic disorder that brings serious physical and developmental challenges to his life. We can only imagine what he's going through and what it's like for his mom and dad and extended family.

In the midst of these challenges, Enoch's dad, Noah, announced he was going to write a book on fatherhood. He wasn't sure when he would find the time to write this book or when it would be published, but he had decided on a memorable and moving title: *Poop, Pee, and Carrots*.

Noah explains that his transition into fatherhood has been characterized by that specific combination of prominent smells. And he says, "No matter how much you scrub, the smell doesn't leave."

Have you been there? We suspect that kind of olfactory image rings true for dads who face similar challenges or have children with special needs.

Noah continued with this nugget: "Being able to accept that smell—and the fact that your wife smells the same—is the glue that holds your family together when times get tough."

Now, we've never heard fatherhood described that way. Also, who knew these three ingredients could be combined to make glue? But isn't that real life for dads? Accepting your role, whether you're in the middle of a challenge or just doing what needs to be done.

For a season, fathering really does revolve around a constant and never-ending succession of dirty diapers. Anything you want to accomplish must take place between diaper changes.

Later seasons are all about getting kids where they need to go. Basketball practice. Church groups. School functions. Play dates with friends. "Taxi dad" is a big part of your role.

When your kids become teenagers, your role might be "Patient dad," or you might be the main character in a book titled *Car Keys, Curfews, and Late-Night Conversations*.

As your kids transition to adulthood, you can follow up with *Where Did the Time Go?* and *What's My Role as a Father Now?* Take heart, Dad—your grown-up kids still need you in their lives.

We totally appreciate Noah's perspective, especially since he's a relatively young dad. If you can accept the situation in which you find yourself and still make the most of every other opportunity to be an involved dad, you will be concocting a powerful glue to bond your family through any and every season.

> *"You know you're a devoted dad when you stop right in the middle of a family outing or activity and say, 'Phew! I should write a book about this!'"*
>
> **—BROCK GRIFFIN**

85

Tough Situations

Here at NCF, we often hear from men who don't have access to their children. They want to be the best dads they can be, but for whatever reason, they are denied that opportunity. For these men, all this talk about loving, coaching, and modeling seems pointless. Frustration overflows. They think, *What's the point if I can't be with my kids?*

Admittedly, the coauthors of this book can't fully relate to what these dads are going through. We do hurt for them. We know it's heartbreaking. And we pledge to continue our research in this area and suggest ways in which these dads can successfully engage their children.

When we hear about custody battles and child-support challenges, it's abundantly clear that we're talking about dads who love their children and are fighting for the chance to be involved fathers. These dads already know there are no easy solutions, but they don't give up.

If you can relate to this situation, we want to offer four pieces of encouragement that probably apply to your situation. If you are facing other challenges, we think you can find ways to apply these also.

Focus on your long-term commitment to your child. That will help see you through the daily ups and downs and the major roadblocks to your fathering.

A good friend of ours was separated from his three kids when they were school-age. After a bitter divorce, he was barred from direct contact with his kids and faced parental alienation. Still he remained steadfast in his faithful and respectful attempts to connect with his children.

And it paid off. The kids grew, and eventually his oldest daughter sought him out on her own and moved in with him. Sometime later, after seven years of separation, his son also expressed a desire to reconnect.

Now, no one wants to go through something like that, but some dads do. An unwavering commitment to maintaining high standards of integrity and faithfulness gives you the best chance of a happy ending.

If you aren't able to be an everyday role model for your kids, focus on your own character. Display sound judgment, respect the needs of others, connect with God and a community of believers, seek accountability, and stay positive in your work and the other areas of life. Your character and reputation will serve as a beacon to draw your children back to you—even if it takes months or years. Yes, it's hard, but it's well worth it.

Find ways to be involved in their lives—respectfully, creatively, and steadfastly.

Of course, the dad who doesn't have access to his children because of his custody agreement will have to live out those principles differently from other dads. If loving the child's mother isn't part of the equation, that dad can at least work on respecting her, cooperating with her, and giving his children access to other people who are modeling healthy relationships.

Maybe the best coaching you can do is through email and texts. Does your child use social networking websites and apps? Use them as a way to connect, especially when you're apart. Or write letters to your child and either mail them or save them for the future.

Years ago, before modern technology, one dad worked on a submarine for 90 days at a time. He prepared by writing postcards to his children for every day of his trip, and he had a friend drop one in the mail each day. He found a way to effectively love, coach, and be a model for his children despite a huge challenge. And you can too.

Maybe you can gain permission to literally be their coach. If your kids are on sports teams, sign up to be an assistant or parent helper.

Or volunteer as a youth leader or Sunday school teacher at the church your kids attend.

Lean on other dads in your situation. You may be a divorced dad, a single dad, an adoptive dad, a stepdad, a traveling dad…maybe even an incarcerated dad. You may just be too busy. Almost all dads struggle at one time or another to find balance in their schedules.

Seek out a dad who's a step or two further along and ask him some questions. "What's working for you? What have you learned? What's the best way you show consistency for your children? What adjustments have you made? What creative solutions have you used to connect with your kids?"

Even though you might feel alone, you're not. Other dads have been through something similar. Reach out to a few other men of good character and start meeting to encourage each other and share ideas.

Pray. Matthew 7:11 says, "If you, then, though you are evil, know how to give good gifts to your children, how much more will your Father in heaven give good gifts to those who ask him!"

Ultimately, for any fathering challenge, we have to stay on our knees. Every day we must remind ourselves that God is the heavenly Father and that he loves our children even more than we do. We need to trust him to faithfully watch over our kids despite our shortcomings or whatever situation may be keeping us from being with them. When we seek God's will for our children in prayer, we're giving them exactly what they need—and we're likely to have more peace about our daily challenges.

Dad, no matter what, don't let frustration get the best of you. Stay close to God. Get the support you need. Remember that other dads in your situation have found ways to stay connected with their kids, and you can do it also.

Finally, a word for any dad who has read this chapter and can't relate to this situation. You live with your kids. You and your wife are committed to each other and look forward to a long future together.

That's all good news. But please, don't take your situation for granted. Don't go on relational cruise control. Be intentional about strengthening your marriage. Be a positive influence in your children's lives every day. Don't let apathy or complacency put you in a situation that leads to the disintegration of your family.

Ask any divorced dad. Walking down the hallway to tuck your kids in at night is much easier than driving across town, or even worse, forfeiting your chance to see them.

> *"Even if a dad can't be with his kids, he's still a dad."*
>
> **—CAREY CASEY**

86

Teens Being Teens

We heard from a dad named Aaron whose 14-year-old son said, "You're the worst dad ever. You don't do anything for me." It was an impulsive statement in the heat of the moment, but that's the kind of thing a dad doesn't forget.

So here's what Aaron did. He gave his son an invoice for all the money he spent on his son during his life. He itemized equipment and team costs for four different sports, trips and vacations, clothing, school supplies, toys, computers, food, and on and on. He also listed "dad's hours," but as he said, there's no price on those.

The total was just under $850,000. We don't know how accurate that is, but we're guessing it's pretty close. We're also guessing the invoice didn't have the desired effect.

Anyone who has been around teenagers for any amount of time will confirm that Aaron's son most likely responded to Aaron's itemized list by becoming even angrier and more defensive. The young man was already exhibiting a bit of teenage petulance, so why would a dad want to pile on? In the end, we cannot recommend Aaron's parenting strategy. As they say on television, "Don't try this at home."

Here's the takeaway: You need to know that many teenagers don't appreciate what they have.

In response to our teens, we dads want to defend ourselves, explain how much we sacrifice on their behalf, and teach our kids a lesson. One obvious impulse would be to take away one privilege and another and another until ungrateful teenagers change their attitude. After all, that's how the real world works—if they smart off to their boss someday, there will be consequences. That sure feels like a lesson worth teaching.

But again, that's not a solution that will bring about any peace or understanding. Like so many fathering challenges, it might help to look at the situation from our child's perspective.

Kids live in the moment. Teenagers may sometimes look like adults and often think they're adults, but they simply don't have information and experience that comes from more than a decade of earning a living, paying bills, and making sacrifices for a family.

You have that benefit. You have the ability to take that long-term view. So when your teenager goes on a "that's not fair" rant, we recommend you respond like an adult. Step back and take a good look a few years down the road. Sometime in their twenties, most young people get a bit wiser and realize how dedicated their parents were and are. So for now, it makes sense for you just to smile, maintain self-control, and continue to do what's best for your entire family, since you are reasonably sure they'll grow out of this immature point of view.

As dads, we have to find that balance between "teaching him a lesson" and maintaining our poise. Sometimes we do need to bring about tough consequences and teach them important lessons. Other times, you'll want to pause and see if you can remember what it was like to be a teenager. In the meantime, thank God that he has given you the maturity, patience, and unconditional love you need to get through this season of parenting.

Hang in there, Dad. It's all worth the effort.

> *"It's a teenager's job to test the waters of adulthood.*
> *It's a dad's job to make sure they don't get in*
> *over their head or swept off by the current."*
>
> **—JAY PAYLEITNER**

87

Wear It for the Kids

Not long ago, a dad we know was in our office, and we couldn't help noticing a pair of socks that didn't really match the rest of his clothes that day. On closer inspection, they turned out to be Superman socks.

Now, we are far from fashion snobs at the National Center for Fathering, so no official reprimand was in order. But we also couldn't leave it alone. What was the story?

It turns out his young son is currently fascinated with superheroes. The boy is really into Superman and Batman, and his dad was wearing those socks simply because he knew it would amuse his son.

We think that's a pretty good reason to wear silly socks.

Brock is big into cycling, and he found out that his daughter Brooklyn shares a name with an Italian racing team from the 1970s and early '80s—Brooklyn Chewing Gum. He went online, and sure enough, that team's jerseys were still available, so he bought one.

Sometimes when he's getting geared up for a ride, he'll come downstairs with that jersey on—featuring his daughter's name printed boldly across the chest. And she smiles. Or when he's wearing a different one, sometimes she'll say, "Dad, how come you're not wearing *my* shirt?"

Maybe you do something similar. You have a T-shirt from a place you visited with your son. Or maybe a necktie or coffee mug or golf towel your daughter gave you as a gift.

We urge you to keep wearing and using those things—even if they clash with your outfit or seem a little silly. More than looking a certain way, you're sending some valuable messages to your child.

"I'm tracking with you. I'm noticing who you are and what you like."

"You're special to me. I enjoy being your dad and letting people know I'm your dad."

"We have a strong connection that I'm proud of."

If your daughter's favorite color is orange or purple, make sure you own an orange or purple tie or dress shirt. Maybe your son picks up on a hobby that's not on your radar, such as skateboarding, NASCAR, or surfing. Find a keychain with an icon from that sport and see how quickly he notices.

For sure, if your daughter makes you a braided twine bracelet, you need to wear it for weeks and weeks and weeks. Probably until it falls off.

When your son or daughter heads off to college, give a hint that you'd love a sweatshirt or T-shirt with the name of their school. The bolder, the better.

So, Dad, go ahead and rock those socks, neckties, shirts, and accessories. Do it loud and proud. Those moments of connection with your child are worth it—even if you get a few double takes when you're out and about. Any looks of surprise will quickly be replaced by smiles when people see that you're just showing your commitment to your kids.

> *"You're the kind of dad who would do anything for your kids, but would you wear anything?"*
>
> **—BROCK GRIFFIN**

88

Omar

In a few of the earlier chapters, we mentioned WATCH D.O.G.S. (Dads of Great Students). It's the innovative educational initiative from NCF in which fathers, stepfathers, grandfathers, and other father figures volunteer for one day a year at their child's school. During their day, WatchDOGS may help kids on and off buses, serve as teachers' helpers, play at recess, monitor the lunchroom, or just about anything the principal and teachers can think of. It typically includes lots of involvement with the kids, which is one of the reasons we love talking about it. There are close to 5000 WatchDOG schools in the United States, and we've made the program easy to start at your child's school. The website fathers.com has all the information you need to get started.

We saved the best WATCH D.O.G.S. story for last. It actually begins in the summer at a local swimming pool. A dad named Omar was in the water enjoying the time with his kids while his wife looked on from poolside. Not far away, a young boy was playing with his sister. Several times Omar heard the sister say, "You're playing too rough with me." The boy replied, "There is no one else."

Omar heard that comment, and it sparked something inside of him. He thought, *Well, if that little guy needs someone to roughhouse with, I can do that.* And roughhouse they did. While Omar splashed and goofed around with his own kids, this other young boy naturally and easily joined the action.

Across the way, Omar's wife was talking with the boy's mother, and the two moms enjoyed the antics displayed by Omar and the kids. It was turning out to be a great afternoon at the park district pool. Between splash attacks, Omar even found a moment to talk with the boy about some of the ways young men need to act—like treating their mothers and sisters with respect and kindness.

Omar later learned that the boy's mom thanked his wife for sharing Omar at the pool. The boy's father was not in the picture, and she knew her son needed some positive role models. Omar was glad he could provide those brief moments of fun and invest a little in his life.

That's the end of the story…until the next fall. As a WatchDOG dad at his son's school, Omar was walking the halls and helping in classrooms when he saw that little boy again. Without any prompting, the boy walked up to Omar and said, "I'm still being good to my sister." Omar says they have bumped into each other at the school several times since.

Dad, please understand that this kind of story—this kind of impact—is what we are all about at NCF.

We want dads to be awesome dads. But we also talk a lot about how we can help fathers and father figures help *other* kids outside the family circle. We know that even little gestures and comments can go a long way. Omar showed that he cared, and those brief moments of interaction at the pool made a lasting impression on that boy. It's heroic stuff!

As Omar wrote to us, "There are children in our community who need us. To any dad out there, please keep your eyes and ears open, and do what comes natural."

Dad, there are other kids around who need your encouragement, your roughhousing, and a healthy dose of Christ's love. In some cases, they may even need a bit of correction or a challenge to be kind and respectful.

We are well aware some might say that in today's culture, Omar went too far. They might insist and warn that strange men should not horse around with kids they meet in parks and pools, giving them life lessons. We understand that concern. We do need to be aware of social cues, personal boundaries, and the legal ramifications of interacting with minors.

But Omar did the right thing. We can't let fear keep us from loving others and helping to build a community. Take a cue from Omar, the awesome roughhousing WatchDOG dad, and do what comes natural.

> *"Three things will last forever—faith, hope, and love—and the greatest of these is love."*
>
> **—1 CORINTHIANS 13:13 NLT**

89

Principles for Parenting Challenges

Not long ago we received this question from a dad: "What's your position on allowing teens to go out on school nights?"

All dads face similar day-to-day challenges and decisions. How much computer or TV time is appropriate for your child? What's the right age to get your child a cell phone? The list of challenges seems endless.

To be honest, at the National Center for Fathering, we don't have official positions on all these. Each child and each situation is unique, so we prefer to talk about the larger principles involved. To illustrate, let's take this dad's question about allowing a teenager to stay out late on a school night.

First we would talk about the importance of a father's awareness. We encourage dads to know their children's interests, strengths, and weaknesses. Some teens are responsible and trustworthy, so being out late once in a while wouldn't be much of an issue. Others are not, so parents would be wise to pull back the reins a bit.

Maybe you've heard this helpful perspective on parenting. Imagine a line graph with a gradual upward slope signifying how a maturing child will gain more freedom and make more consequential decisions as the parent's role diminishes. As kids grow in responsibility, they gain more freedom and earn more trust. At the same time, a parent's role gradually moves from mostly *control and direction* to being more of an *influence*.

For example, when kids first enter high school, parents should insist that they take a challenging course load, including classes they may not be excited about. But each semester, they should also be given freedom to choose one or two electives on their own. That will help prepare them for shouldering more critical decisions in a few short years, such as choosing a college and a major.

Our awareness as parents helps us decide what our kids can handle. Some middle schoolers could be given $20 on Monday to cover lunch for the entire week. Other kids in the same class would blow it all before the end of the first day. One young teenager may be responsible enough to feed the family dog. Another child the same age shouldn't be trusted to keep a goldfish alive.

When it comes to school-night activities, there are other matters to consider—what the child will be doing, whom they are with, and so on. Here's a valid thought process to consider: *If I believe the event is good for my child, such as something that will nurture his faith, then I want him to be there—even if it means a late night and even if he might be tired at school the next day. Some things are worth that. But if he's just going to see a movie or hang with friends, that's a different story.*

It's not a cop-out for us to say it's impossible to make specific recommendations that cover all the variables. But we can encourage you to know your children. Consider their history. Be optimistic. Keep the big picture in mind. And remember each child is different.

Challenging questions are good motivators to get with your wife and review your basic principles for parenting. Be willing to make adjustments as your children grow and change.

And sometimes, invite your children in on that conversation.

> *"Being a parent would be much easier if you didn't have to deal with children."*
>
> **—JAY PAYLEITNER**

90

Dave Takes His Daughter Shopping

Once upon a time, Dave took his preteen daughter out to shop for clothes.

Sounds like the beginning of a frightening horror story, doesn't it? For many dads and daughters, going shopping for clothes might seem like sticking sharp objects under your fingernails. For both of you! It's asking for trouble, especially since father-daughter relationships can go through extended months of misunderstanding, tension, and lack of communication.

Well, life—and shopping—with your daughter doesn't have to be that way. As a matter of fact, a few hours in a mall with your favorite young lady might be a springboard for a new season of growth and communication in your relationship.

Maybe that's why we like Dave's approach so much. It was no major shopping spree—just updating some things his daughter had outgrown. Dave looked at the afternoon as an opportunity for the two of them to learn something about each other and to throw in a life lesson or two.

For example, he gave her a budget. She could spend only a certain amount, which forced her to make smart buying decisions. Should she get two pairs of jean shorts or one more expensive pair? It was the kind of decision adults make all the time, and Dave let his daughter know she was capable of making it.

At one point, Dave asked his daughter if it was awkward to have him there helping her pick out her clothes. She looked at him and beamed. "No, I love it!"

Also, since they were summer clothes, Dave had the opportunity to give input about what's appropriate for a girl to wear. Make no mistake—it's appropriate and even essential for dads to be proactive in this area and intentional about influencing daughters toward modesty. We all know what guys are thinking when they see young ladies in revealing outfits, and we need to talk to our daughters about that. That might include telling her, "You're sending a message you don't want to send."

Don't have the conversation in the store. But later, in the car or over ice cream, a dad should be able to talk with his daughter about what scenarios may unfold when a woman flaunts her body or doesn't respect herself. Dad, you are exactly the right person to address those issues with your daughter.

Dads play an important role in modeling the kind of behavior their daughters should expect from young men. We also play a leading role in establishing and affirming our family's values and our obedience to God's Word—regardless of what our culture may say is right or is in style.

So even though these aren't always easy discussions, we dads can have them if we keep our cool and focus on expressing love and concern instead of fear or anger.

Other topics of discussion on your shopping trip might be about making your own choices and not being forced to follow fashion trends. Also, as you're walking among the racks of women's clothing, you might ask your daughter's advice on what kind of things you should buy your bride for her next birthday or an upcoming holiday.

It was just a simple shopping trip, but we applaud Dave's commitment to his daughter. It's a reminder that as our daughters grow up, we need to be intentional about spending time in their world, doing what they want and discovering what's important to them. If we bring the right attitude, then like Dave's daughter, our girls will love spending that time with us.

"The surest way to spend time with your kids and learn what makes them tick is to do stuff they want to do."

—BROCK GRIFFIN

91

Work Works

As we interview dads for our Father of the Year contests, one of our follow-up questions is, "How does your work impact your ability to be a dad?"

In their response, the men sometimes express regret or apologize that work gets in the way of their role as a father. They suggest that long hours on the job, travel schedules, and other work responsibilities are preventing them from being the best dad they can be.

We understand where these dads are coming from. It's hard to miss your kids' games, concerts, and outings. Committed dads want to have dinner with their family and tuck the kids in every night. But here at NCF we want to make it very clear that we believe work is honorable, valuable, and even heroic. A man providing for his family is a beautiful thing.

We've given it much thought and talked to a lot of dads regarding the challenge of balancing work and family, and we've identified a few unspoken truths that you may not have previously considered.

Work is a privilege. As children get older, they understand that everyone has a job to do in the family. Groceries have to be purchased. Dinner has to be cooked. Dishes have to be washed. Carpets have to be vacuumed. Homework has to be done. No matter what the task, it really is a privilege to contribute to the family, and every member of the family has something to contribute.

Work shouldn't be presented as a miserable experience. Even if you hate your job, please don't bring that attitude home with you. Sure, you're going to have frustrations once in a while. Overtime, lost promotions, downsizing, lost clients, obnoxious bosses…these are part of just about everyone's working career. Still, there's honor in work. A setback on the job is one more reason to find joy and meaning in your family and your faith. Plus, when your kids begin to settle into their own calling, you want them to seek and find a career that matches their gifts and passions. Working our sweet spot and doing something we love makes on-the-job frustrations a lot easier to take. That's true for your kids—and for you.

Work leads to new skills that make you a better father. This truth comes from a dad named Rudy who responded to our question about how his work impacts his family. He said work does impact his ability to be a dad…but in a positive way.

Rudy described how his job has taught him about teamwork, communication, cooperation, and the value of establishing and meeting goals and expectations. He explains that many of those principles can be applied to leading and managing our families. He's got a point.

At work, regular staff meetings keep everyone updated on what's going on and remind workers about the company's main goals and vision. At home, family meetings or councils are a great idea for the same reasons.

On the job site, managers give direction and set expectations for everyone—and we dads do the same thing. A good manager will have an open door for staff members who have issues or need help with something—just like a good dad.

Because of our jobs, we know about workplace dynamics and the challenge of dealing with different personalities. Your colleagues at work have unique skill sets and various roles to help the organization achieve its goals. Well, there's a lot of that when you're leading a family too.

Rudy said that he also applies the idea of an annual theme or slogan to his family, which promotes family unity and helps keep them focused on a bigger goal. That's another great idea. You could use a Bible verse the whole family learns and repeats throughout the year, starting in January or when the school year begins.

Dad, we don't know what your role is at your job. Maybe you're a stay-at-home dad. But whatever experience you have in the business world, take the best lessons you've learned there and use them to help lead your family in a positive direction.

> "Whatever you do, work at it with all your heart, as working for the Lord, not for human masters."
>
> **—COLOSSIANS 3:23**

92

The Fatherhood Crisis

Did you know that more than 20 million children live apart from their biological fathers? That's around 33 percent of all children in our land, and there are tragic consequences.

Fatherless children are much more likely to live in poverty, have emotional and behavioral problems, drop out of school, commit suicide, suffer physical and mental disorders, commit criminal acts, engage in premarital sex, get pregnant, and use drugs and alcohol.

The National Center for Fathering has become a trusted resource for statistics and primary research on fathering. You can dig deep and see the staggering numbers at www.fathers.com/research. The latest research contains some good news and some not-so-good news. But it always points to the critical need for dads to stick around and be directly involved in the lives of their children.

We talk about these things all the time, but it never gets old because we're not counting things. We're talking about the well-being of our children...more than 20 million kids facing tough odds in many areas of life. That isn't to say all of them will struggle. Many of these kids will end up in loving adoptive homes, and many stepdads are getting the job done heroically. We applaud single moms who are doing the best they can, and we're not saying that life for their children is guaranteed to be a mess. But we are talking about giving all kids the best chance possible.

Think about other crises we see in the news. If a disease affected 20 million kids or a natural disaster threatened that many children, there would be worldwide outrage, and public figures would be urging everyone to take action. Our leaders would rally all of us to "save the children, our most precious resource." It would be that kind of emergency.

Unfortunately, there just isn't that kind of urgency about the fatherhood crisis. Maybe people have learned to expect less of fathers and just deal with the fact that so many dads aren't there, so they think it's no big deal.

But this is a big deal, and we believe God has called the National Center for Fathering to carry this message. And now that you know, we believe you are also part of the solution.

Together let's get the word out. When you find yourself in one of those downer conversations about what's wrong with America, go ahead and state the facts: "Maybe it's because more than 20 million kids are growing up without their biological fathers."

Then let's not linger on the negative. Rather than beat up on fathers who aren't there, let's try to keep it positive. Here are a few phrases you can inject in your everyday conversations and digital communications. They're not slogans. They're not clever. They're just true.

"Dads are important."

"Kids need dads."

"I love my kids."

"An involved dad makes a huge difference for families."

"Children are a gift from God."

"It's great being a dad."

The root cause of the fatherhood crisis may really just be a widespread attitude that dads don't matter. The best way to fight this battle might *not* be with giant rallies, government policies, or million-dollar ad campaigns. This battle might be fought and won at the grassroots level.

Let's start by being the best dads we can. Not perfect, just involved and invested. Then let's encourage and support other dads in our circle of influence. Let's do everything we can to inspire and empower the next generation of dads. Finally, let's make sure we use positive words to elevate the noble calling of fatherhood.

> *"The best way to help single moms is to have fewer single moms."*
>
> **—JAY PAYLEITNER**

93

God the Father

Do you ever just sit and marvel at your kids? As we mentioned in the introduction, the three coauthors have a total of 12 kids, and they're growing up at an incredible rate. Carey and Jay also have grandkids, which takes the wonderment to an entirely new level.

Like many dads, we sometimes look at our families and say, "How did this happen?" These children of ours are turning into good people—successful students, committed spouses, dedicated employees, church members, parents, and basically good citizens. Because our kids exist, the world is a better place.

Then of course, because we have egos, we begin to take credit for our children's awesomeness. *Hey, world! Look what I did!* Oops. That is just a foolish, misguided notion.

On days when we're smart, we give a ton of credit to our brides, Melanie Casey, Tara Griffin, and Rita Payleitner. God blessed us with wives who encourage us as dads. These gifted women bring their own passion and wisdom to their roles as mothers and hold us accountable when we need to step it up as spiritual leaders of our families.

Then, on days when we're *really* smart, we realize what's actually going on. We look at our kids, see the things they're pursuing, their gifts and achievements, and we finally realize we didn't do that.

Even the most committed dads and moms should never take credit for their children's abilities and accomplishments. It's a God thing.

Being humbled and saying that right out loud conveys exactly the right attitude for every dad.

Even if you were a professional athlete, you didn't give your child that speed, agility, and competitive heart. God did.

If you're a concert pianist, world-class chef, or nuclear physicist, you may have introduced your child to music, the culinary arts, or science. But it's God who makes our kids who they are.

If your child faces and overcomes a tremendous life challenge, your love and support were critical. But the glory goes to God.

All 12 of our kids are unique. Christie, Patrice, Marcellus, and Chance. Alec, Randall, Max, Isaac, and Rae Anne. Cole, Brooklyn, and Devan. They may be like us in a few ways, but they are their own individuals. They're living souls on loan to us for a season as we take care of them, but they really do belong to their Creator.

Just to confirm what you already know. Each of your kids is unique. Even if you named them Junior. Even if they follow in your exact career path. Even if you have a pair of identical twins. God has a special and carefully chosen plan for each son and daughter of every dad who reads this book. And that plan is very likely something beyond your imagination.

Are you humbled yet? Consider this. What's happening in the lives of our children extends far beyond our own ability and power. Once we realize that core truth, we can embrace an even more astounding fact: God is their Father even more than we are.

That's one more reason we need to be understanding when our children don't follow the path we envision for them. Bottom line, who they become is less about us and more about our heavenly Father.

If you are a younger dad, you would do well to embrace this fact sooner rather than later. Your fathering will go more smoothly and you'll be less stressed if you trust God to shape and lead your children. Do your very best, Dad. But let our heavenly Father take the lead in their lives.

If you look for it, you will see evidence of God at work in the life of your son or daughter. When that happens, just smile and praise God for what he's doing. And be grateful for the privilege of being part of his plan.

> *"So if you sinful people know how to give good gifts to your children, how much more will your heavenly Father give good gifts to those who ask him?"*
>
> **—MATTHEW 7:11 NLT**

Notes

1. Penelope Trunk, "Hold CEOs accountable for their bad parenting" (blog post), June 20, 2007, blog.penelopetrunk.com/2007/06/20/hold-ceos-accountable-for-their-bad-parenting/.
2. University of Rochester Medical Center, "Nearly One-Third of U.S. Parents Don't Know What to Expect of Infants," *ScienceDaily*, May 4, 2008, www.sciencedaily.com/releases/2008/05/080504095631.htm.
3. Tyler Chernesky, "No place like home for the holidays," *Indiana Daily Student*, November 28, 2010, www.idsnews.com/article/2010/11/no-place-like-home-for-the-holidays?id=78715.
4. Cited in Reuters, "TheBump.com and ForbesWoman.com Co-Parenting Survey Reveals Nearly 1 in 5 Working and Stay-at-Home Mothers Feel Like 'Married Single Moms,'" June 15, 2011, in.reuters.com/article/2011/06/15/idUS151252+15-Jun-2011+BW20110615.

BOOKS BY CAREY CASEY

Championship Fathering

The 21-Day Dad's Challenge (general editor)

★

BOOKS BY JAY PAYLEITNER

52 Things Kids Need from a Dad

52 Things to Pray for Your Kids

Once Upon a Tandem

The One Year Life Verse Devotional

52 Things Wives Need from Their Husbands

52 Things Husbands Need from Their Wives

365 Ways to Say "I Love You" to Your Kids

One-Minute Devotions for Dads

52 Things Daughters Need from Their Dads

52 Things Sons Need from Their Dads

10 Conversations Kids Need to Have with Their Dad

What If God Wrote Your Bucket List?

52 Ways to Connect as a Couple

**National Center
for Fathering**

Engaging fathers. Enriching lives.

The National Center for Fathering (NCF) is a nonprofit 501(c)3 organization with the mission of improving the lives of children and establishing a positive fathering and family legacy that will impact future generations by inspiring and equipping fathers and father figures to be actively engaged in the life of every child. The research is clear: Children thrive when they have an involved father or father figure—someone who loves them, knows them, guides them, and helps them achieve their destiny. NCF is dedicated to reversing the negative trends of fatherlessness. We focus our work in four key areas.

Research. At the core of NCF's work is the Championship Fathering Profile, a proprietary assessment tool that helps men understand their strengths and opportunities to improve as a father. Developed by a team of researchers, this profile provides insights for fathers and serves as the benchmark for evaluating the effectiveness of our father-training programs. NCF maintains continued interest in expanding the knowledge base of the fathering field.

Training. NCF offers training through seminars, small groups, and training programs. We have reached more than 80,000 fathers through our seminars and have equipped more than 1,000 trainers to provide our research-based father training in their local communities.

Programming. NCF provides impactful and meaningful fathering programs that enrich the lives of fathers, children, and families. WATCH D.O.G.S. (Dads of Great Students), our flagship program, is currently in 46 states, four countries and more than 4,700 schools. Find out more about WATCH D.O.G.S. at www.fathers.com. NCF also provides the "What My Father Means to Me" essay contest, a Father of the Year celebration, and other programs.

Resources. NCF's website provides a wealth of free resources for dads in nearly every fathering situation. Dads can receive a weekly e-mail full of fathering ideas, advice, and inspiration. NCF offers free e-books to help dads tackle their fathering situations. We also have a daily radio program featuring Carey Casey that airs on more than 350 stations. Daily tips and updates are also posted to our NCF social media platforms. For more information, please visit www.fathers.com.

★

Carey Casey is chief executive officer of the Kansas City–based National Center for Fathering. He's the author of *Championship Fathering* and the general editor of *The 21-Day Dad's Challenge*. Carey has served as chaplain for the Kansas City Chiefs, the Dallas Cowboys (under Hall of Fame Coach Tom Landry), and other NFL teams. He was also chaplain for the US Olympic team at the 1988 Summer Games in Seoul, South Korea. Carey was also co-pastor of a church in inner-city Chicago and spent 18 years in various roles with the Fellowship of Christian Athletes. Since 2009, Carey has served on the White House Task Force on Fatherhood and Healthy Families, and in June of 2012, he was selected as a "Fatherhood Champion of Change" as part of President Obama's "Winning the Future" initiative. Carey also serves as a member of the National Fatherhood Leaders Group, which promotes responsible fatherhood policy, research, advocacy, and practice. Carey and his wife, Melanie, have four children and nine grandchildren.

Brock Griffin is writing and publications director at the National Center for Fathering. He has been with NCF since 1991. Brock handles or helps with many writing and editing projects for NCF, including books, blogs, *Today's Father Weekly* e-mails, and articles for outside publications. He also collaborates with Carey Casey to produce content for *Today's Father*, Carey's three-minute radio program that began in 1993 and now airs on more than 400 stations worldwide. Brock and his wife, Tara, have three children and live in the Kansas City area.

Jay Payleitner, one of the top freelance Christian radio producers in the United States, has worked on *Josh McDowell Radio*, *Today's Father*, *Jesus Freaks Radio* for the Voice of the Martyrs, *Project Angel Tree* with Chuck Colson, and many others. He's also a popular speaker on parenting and marriage and the author of a dozen-plus books, including the bestselling *52 Things Kids Need from a Dad* and *What If God Wrote Your Bucket List?* He is also creator of *The Dad Manifesto* poster and book. Jay has served as an AWANA director, a wrestling coach, the executive director of the Illinois Fatherhood Initiative, and an affiliate of the National Center for Fathering. Jay and his wife, Rita, live near Chicago, where they've raised five great kids and loved on ten foster babies. Best of all, Jay is a new Gramps!